ISLAM

Jan

GCSE Religious Studies

Hodder & Stoughton

A MEMBER OF THE HODDER HEADLINE GROUP

OCR

RECOGNISING ACHIEVEMENT

ACKNOWLEDGEMENTS

The author and publishers thank the following for permission to reproduce copyright photographs in this book:

Peter Sanders, pp iv, v, 2, 3, 4, 6, 9, 11, 13, 14, 22, 23, 26, 27btm, 39, 40, 42, 44, 47, 48, 52, 53, 54, 55, 56, 57, 58, 65, 66, 67, 68 top and bottom, 69, 70, 72, 73, 75, 76, 82, 84, 85, 86, 88, 89, 93, 94, 99, 101, 102, 104, 106, 107, 113; Christine Osborne, pp 27top, 28, 31, 37, 90; Camerapix/Christine Osborne Pictures, p46; Ta Ha Publishers Ltd, p5; David H. Wells/CORBIS p8; Lindsay Hebberd/CORBIS, p29, Reuters NewMedia Inc./CORBIS, p31, Christine Osborne/CORBIS, p43, Bettmann/CORBIS, p62, Robert van der Hilst/CORBIS, p64, Jeremy Horner/CORBIS, p91, Wally McNamee/CORBIS, p112; The Bridgeman Art Library, Collection of Andrew McIntosh Patrick, UK, Bird's eye view of Mecca, 1784 engraving, p10; NASA, p 25; The World Federation, Islamic Centre, p41; Sonia Halliday Photographs/F.H.C. Birch, p68 centre; Ronald Grant Archive, p110, PA Photos pp115, 116; Digital Entertainment Ltd, p118; Islamic Relief, p119.

by kind permission of the Alliance of Religions and Conservation.

have been inadvertently overlooked, the publishers will be pleased to make

AUTHOR'S NOTES

The transliteration of Arabic words in the text is based on the SCAA Glossary 1994 and *A Popular Dictionary of Islam*, I R Netton, Curzon Press, London, 1992.

The Arabic letters 'ayn and hamza are transliterated throughout as ' and ' respectively.

All quotations from the Qur'an are taken from *The Meaning of the Holy Qur'an*, 'Abdullah Yusuf 'Ali, 7th ed., Amana Publications, Beltsville, 1995.

This Arabic 'logo-type' is composed of the words *'Salla-illahu alaihi wa sallam'* – 'peace and blessings of Allah upon him'. They are used by Muslims every time the Prophet Muhammad is mentioned. This phrase is sometimes written as 'SAW' or the words 'Peace be upon him' (pbuh) are used. Similar respect is given to the other Prophets.

Dates in this book are given as:

CE = Common Era

BCE = Before the Common Era

AH = Anno Hegirae (see page 12)

Orders: please contact Bookpoint Ltd, 130 Milton Park, Abingdon, Oxon OX14 4SB.
Telephone: (44) 01235 827720, Fax: (44) 01235 400454.
Lines are open from 9.00 – 6.00, Monday to Saturday, with a 24 hour message answering service.
Email address: orders@bookpoint.co.uk

British Library Cataloguing in Publication Data
A catalogue record for this title is available from The British Library

ISBN 0 340 78963 8

First published 2001
Impression number   10 9 8 7 6 5 4 3 2 1
Year   2005 2004 2003 2002 2001

Cover photo from Photodisk
Typeset by Wyvern 21, 277 Bath Road, Bristol BS4 3EH
Printed in Italy for Hodder & Stoughton Educational, a division of Hodder Headline Plc, 338 Euston Road, London NW1 3BH

CONTENTS

INTRODUCTION

Islam is estimated to be the second largest and the fastest growing religion in the modern world, with over eight hundred million followers. Islam, like Judaism and Christianity, originated in the Middle East and is a monotheistic religion. This means that the followers of the religion believe in one God.

Allah is the Arabic word for God. The word 'Islam' means 'submission' and the followers of Islam are called Muslims, people who have submitted themselves to the will of Allah.

As with most religions, Islam is a way of life. Beliefs are intended to affect behaviour and behaviour is expected to reflect beliefs.

When studying the beliefs and practices that make a way of life, many of the topics will interrelate.

It is important to realise that different groups in a religion may emphasise varied aspects of the faith and that individual believers may be at different stages of spiritual growth and awareness. Most religions include a range of people: from nominal members, without any real sense of commitment, to devout followers, who make their beliefs the focus of their lives. That is why it is important to try to avoid stereotypes and generalisations.

The name Allah in Arabic

Muslims live in all parts of the world

- What do you already know about Islam? Work alone for a few minutes then in twos or threes. Compare your notes. Check for possible stereotypes and generalisations. Look again at your notes later in the course and see if your opinions have changed.
- Start a folder labelled 'Islam: A Way of Life' for collecting material from the media about Muslims.
- Make a note to remind yourself to put BCE (Before the Common Era) or CE (Common Era) after all historical dates when you are writing about Islam. Muslims begin their numbering of the years from an event which took place in the year 622 CE and which you can read about on page 12

BELIEFS

The beliefs of Muslims in relation to the following:
- one compassionate creator God;
- the day of Judgement and life after death;
- the life and teaching of Muhammad ﷺ;
- the practice of the Five Pillars and Jihad.

The ways in which these beliefs might affect the lifestyles and outlooks of Muslims in the modern world.

A Muslim is one who submits to Allah and who has made the following declaration of faith:

La ilaha illal lahu muhammadur rasulul lah
There is no god but Allah, Muhammad ﷺ is the messenger of Allah.

This statement of belief is the *Shahadah*, the first of the Five Pillars of Islam on which all the other pillars and the whole faith rests.

The call to prayer, the *Adhan*, has the same theme:

Allah is the Greatest

Allah is the Greatest

Allah is the Greatest

Allah is the Greatest

I bear witness that there is no god but Allah

I bear witness that there is no god but Allah

I bear witness that Muhammad ﷺ is Allah's messenger

I bear witness that Muhammad ﷺ is Allah's messenger

Rush to prayer

Rush to prayer

Rush to success

Rush to success

Allah is the Greatest

Allah is the Greatest

There is no god but Allah

This call is used at the birth and at the death of a Muslim; they should be the first and the last words that a Muslim hears.

It is clear from the Shahadah and the call to prayer that, for Muslims, Allah is not only the central idea of their faith but also the starting point of their beliefs.

The call to prayer should be the first words that a Muslim baby hears

A Muslim burial

ONE COMPASSIONATE CREATOR GOD

In our modern world there are some people who do not believe in the existence of God or gods; but for most religious people, belief in a creator is the starting point of their faith. All people wonder about the answers to questions such as, 'How did the world begin?' 'Why are we here?' and 'What is life all about?' Science provides some answers, but these ultimate questions also provoke religious responses just as they have continued to do throughout human history. Nowadays, we realise that you cannot expect to prove beliefs in the way in which you might check a mathematical fact or a scientific formula. Beliefs are a matter of faith.

STUDY THIS PASSAGE

Read the passage below which is the first surah (chapter) of the Qur'an, the holy book of Muslims. From this chapter, describe what Allah is like and what Allah can do.

In the name of Allah, Most Gracious, Most Merciful,
Praise be to Allah, the Cherisher and Sustainer of the Worlds,
Most Gracious, Most Merciful;
Master of the Day of Judgement,
Thee do we worship,
And Thine aid we seek.
Show us the straight way.
The way of those on whom Thou hast bestowed Thy Grace,
Those whose (portion)
Is not wrath,
And who go not astray.

Al-Fatihah, 'The Opening'
  (Surah 1)

Muslims believe that Allah is the designer and creator of the universe. Not only is Allah the creator but the sole creator. Allah has no partner and no son. The idea of *Tawhid*, the oneness and unity of Allah, is very important to Muslims and was a significant part of the message of Muhammad ﷺ.

Muslims believe that Allah is not only the creator but also the sustainer of the universe who keeps it going. Allah did not just make the universe then ignore it; he rules and controls everything.

For people who believe in a creator God, it is natural to wonder about the character or nature of God. If there is a God – one God, who created the universe – what is this one God like? Is God a tyrant? Is God a bully? Muslims believe that God is compassionate. To be compassionate is to be kind and merciful, but also to be just and fair.

Muslims do not make pictures nor any statue, image or likeness of Allah. This is to avoid the danger of idolatry and because Allah is far beyond human imagination and cannot be compared to anything or anyone else.

No vision can grasp Him, but His grasp is over all vision: He is above all comprehension, yet is acquainted with all things.

(Surah 6:103)

Muslims emphasise the transcendence of Allah and his supreme greatness, which they regard with respect and awe. Muslims believe, also, in the immanence (all-pervading power and presence) of Allah. He cares for even the smallest part of his creation. He is immanent in the simplest matters of daily life. Muslims believe that the natural world, and even the smallest things in it, can point people towards Allah.

A tasbih is a set of 99 prayer beads which helps a Muslim show devotion to Allah by remembering and reciting the 99 names of Allah.

No words can describe Allah properly nor explain about him but Muslims believe that the Qur'an was given in Arabic to Muhammad ﷺ as a special revelation about Allah and the purpose of creation.

Surah 1 shows some of the aspects and characteristics of Allah which are revealed to humans. These characteristics are sometimes called the attributes of Allah or the names of Allah:

The most beautiful names belong to Allah: so call on him by them.

The Qur'an says that Allah has 99 different names.

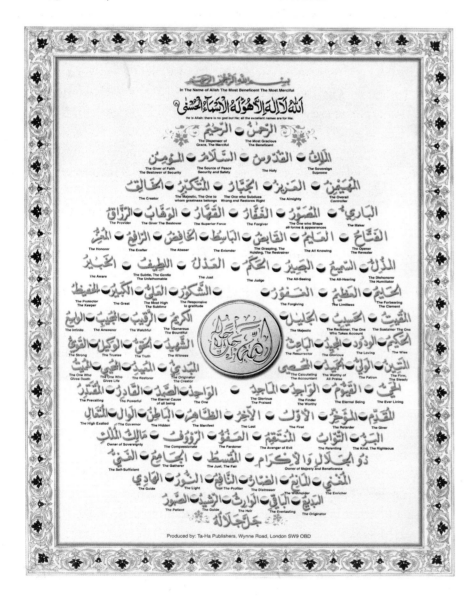

The 99 beautiful names of Allah

According to legend there is one more name but this secret hundredth name is known only to the camel. The Qur'an says that every creature *'knows its own (mode of) prayer and praise'* (Surah 24:41) and that the purpose of creation is to praise Allah.

FOR DISCUSSION

- Find out what is meant by 'transcendence' and 'immanence'? Why might these two ideas be helpful in thinking about beliefs?
- Why is the idea of 'revelation' important for religious people?
- Suggest global issues which you think Muslims might be concerned about and explain why.
- Read The Muslim Declaration on Religion and Nature (on page 18) which was made at Assisi during the Interfaith Ceremony at the World Wildlife Fund's 25th Anniversary celebrations in 1986. How far do you agree with the attitudes expressed in the declaration?

ICT FOR RESEARCH

Visit the web-site of IFEES, the Islamic Foundation for Ecology and Environmental Science, which brings Muslims together to link with other environmental agencies. Find out about their work in support of The Ohito Declaration on Religions, Land and Conservation, which followed The Assisi Declaration in 1995.

A Muslim at prayer

THE DAY OF JUDGEMENT AND LIFE AFTER DEATH

The Qur'an tells Muslims about the nature of God (what Allah is like) and about the power of God (what Allah can do). One of the 99 names is The Omnipotent, which means that Allah has the power to do anything.

Obviously this raises some other important religious questions. If Allah is so powerful and cares so much, then how does Islam explain the existence of evil and suffering?

Muslims believe that Allah's creation was perfect. This perfect creation included other unseen worlds besides the physical natural universe and other beings besides humans and animals. Among these beings are Mala'ikah – angels or messengers of Allah – who have no freewill and no physical bodies, though they can take on human shape.

In Islam, besides angels there are other beings: the jinn. These are spirits usually described as being made of fire and, like humans, they can be good or evil. The chief jinn is Iblis, known also as the devil or Shaytan. Iblis is the author of evil.

Iblis is a jinn who disobeyed Allah but is allowed to tempt humans till the Day of Judgement. Then Iblis will be judged too. This explanation of evil points to a very important conviction: that, however bad things may seem in the world, good is more powerful than evil and, in the end, good is certain to win.

Allah made Mala'ikah from divine light but he created Adam, the first human, from clay. Allah ordered the angels and Jinn to bow down to Adam. The angels obeyed but Iblis refused.

> *(Allah) said: 'O Iblis! What is your reason for not being amongst those who prostrated themselves?' (Iblis) said: 'I am not one to prostrate myself to man whom Thou didst create from sounding clay, from mud moulded into shape.' (Allah) said: 'Then get thee out from here, for thou art rejected, accursed. And the Curse shall be on thee till the Day of Judgement.'*
>
> (Surah 15:32–35)

The Muslim belief that Allah is the sole creator leads to other important concepts.

Allah began the universe and Allah will end the universe. This means that Allah controls everything. Allah gives life and Allah takes it away.

> *Nor can a soul die except by Allah's leave.* (Surah 3:145)

Allah is the Lord of History and Allah will be the Judge of all people at the end of time.

Muslims believe that this life is a preparation for the next life, *akhirah*, life after death. By words like 'the next life' and 'the afterlife' Muslims do **not** mean re-incarnation. Muslims believe that we have only this one life on earth and in it we are tested. Surah 1 refers to the straight path believers are to follow if they are to escape punishment on *Yawmuddin*, the Last Day, the Day of Judgement.

> *Every man's fate we have fastened on his own neck: on the Day of Judgement we shall bring out for him a scroll, which he will see spread open.*
>
> (Surah 17:13)

The fact that every individual is responsible for his or her actions implies another important belief: that humans have been created with freewill. People are free to choose to follow or reject the teachings of Islam but they must face the consequences of their decision at the Last Judgement. At first it seems difficult to reconcile the idea of free will with the complete control that Allah has over everything. In fact Muslims so often say *'In Sha'a Allah'* – if Allah wills – that people outside the faith think of Muslims as fatalistic and they find *Qadar* (Predestination) hard to understand.

FOR DISCUSSION

Beliefs about angels are found in other religions besides Islam and they even appear in the popular media. What names of angels have you heard?

Sometimes the idea of Predestination is described as being like a game of chess. The players can see the moves as the game progresses and they can think ahead to some of the strategies to deal with the possibilities. A chess master can see further ahead than most people and predict the outcome of the game. Allah is omniscient; he knows everything. Allah has no restrictions and can see both past and future. The players have their freedom to make their moves in the game of life but the plans of Allah anticipate and incorporate what he knows is going to happen. This is Predestination by Foreknowledge. Allah is also more caring than we can imagine. Muslims trust Allah to know best and to do what is best for them.

Muslims do not believe in the immortality of the soul but in the resurrection of the body at the Last Day. The soul and the body of each Muslim will be reunited and all the believers will be raised from their graves.

The Day of Judgement and life after death are described in the last two sections of Surah 39. The description tells how there will be the sound of a trumpet, then everything will stop and people will fall down as if unconscious. The trumpet will sound again, heaven and earth will be transformed and the dead will rise to join the living.

The Qur'an warns that when the Last Judgement occurs it will be too late for people to repent. The truth will be so obvious that there will be no opportunity to choose to believe with your own freewill in Allah.

The Qur'an describes the rewards for believers and the punishments for unbelievers. Believers will experience *al-Janna* (paradise) which is like a beautiful peaceful garden full of flowers and birds but unbelievers will have to face dreadful torments in the fires of Hell, *Jahannam*.

The afterlife is really beyond human imagination as both places belong to a totally different dimension from the present world, but one thing is certain about the afterlife: it lasts forever. It is not surprising, therefore, that belief in an afterlife can influence the behaviour of believers in their present life.

THE TEACHING OF MUHAMMAD ﷺ

I believe in Allah, in his angels, in his books, in his messengers, in the Last Day, and in the fact that everything, good or bad, is decided by Allah, the almighty, and in life after death.

This summary of the basic beliefs of Islam is contained in the Al-Imanul Mufassal. It is based on parts of the Qur'an such as Surah 2:285 which lists belief in Allah, his angels, his books and his messengers, and Surah 4:136 which also includes these plus the Day of Judgement. The lists of beliefs of Islam always include Rusulullah, the messengers of Allah. The Shahadah and the call to prayer both refer in particular to the prophet Muhammad ﷺ.

Muslims do not worship Muhammad ﷺ. The importance of Muhammad ﷺ for Muslims is that he is revered as the final messenger bringing the revelation of the actual words of Allah.

Muslims believe that Allah communicates with humans through angels and through prophets. The first Muslim and the first prophet was Adam. He was the first human to be created and his task was to look after the world. Allah told Adam what to do but the message became distorted and other messengers had to be given the words of Allah again.

The main prophets are Nuh (Noah), Ibrahim (Abraham), Musa (Moses), Dawud (David) and 'Isa (Jesus), peace be unto them.

Muslim	Judaeo-Christian
Adam	Adam
Idris	Enoch
Nuh	Noah
Hud	
Salih	
Ibrahim	Abraham
Isma'il	Ishmael
Ishaq	Isaac
Lut	Lot
Ya'qub	Jacob
Yusuf	Joseph
Shu'aib	
Ayyub	Job
Musa	Moses
Harun	Aaron
Dhu'l-kifl	Ezekiel
Dawud	David
Sulamain	Solomon
Ilas	Elias
Al-Yasa'	Elisha
Yunus	Jonah
Zakariyya	Zechariah
Yahya	John
'Isa	Jesus
Muhammad	

According to Muhammad ﷺ there were over 124,000 prophets, but only the 25 listed above are mentioned in the Qur'an.

All the prophets brought the same message. They called the people to worship Allah as the one true God.

Despite the prophets, the message continued to be ignored or distorted. Muhammad ﷺ was the last prophet and received the final revelation from God. He is sometimes called the 'Seal of the Prophets'.

The Qur'an was revealed to Muhammad ﷺ by the Angel Jibril over a period of twenty-three years. Because Muhammad could not read or write, he memorised the Qur'an as he heard it and then dictated it to his secretary Zaid Bin Thabit. It was not compiled as one book until after his death. Since then it has remained unchanged and Muslims say that it cannot be translated from the original Arabic into any other language because that would change the words of Allah.

The first verses of the Qur'an given to the Prophet stress the importance of the message of God and the fact that Muhammad ﷺ was to repeat them so that they can be learnt and recited off by heart.

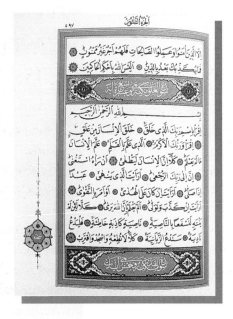

Iqra (Recite)

Surah 96

The final revelation was made shortly before the Prophet's death:

> *Today I have perfected your religion for you, completed my favour upon you, and have chosen for you Islam as your religion.*
>
> (Surah 5:3)

Makkah and the Ka'bah

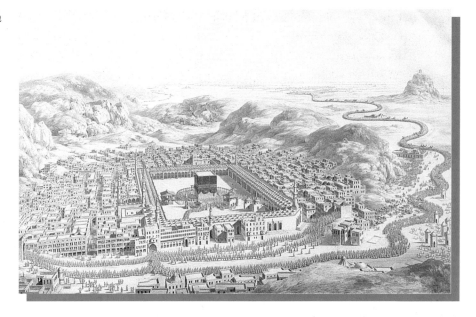

THE LIFE OF MUHAMMAD ﷺ

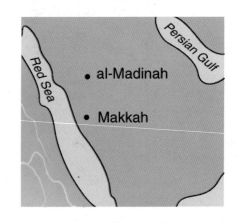

Muhammad ﷺ was born in 570 CE in Makkah, which is now in Saudi Arabia. Makkah was a prosperous city at the centre of a thriving caravan trade and it was also a place of pilgrimage because at the centre was the shrine called the Ka'bah. The name means 'cube' because of the shape. In the corner is set the Black Stone, a meteorite which had been revered by the tribes living in that region for centuries. Muslims believe the Ka'bah was built by the prophet Ibrahim about 4,000 years ago.

The people of Makkah at that time were polytheists: they worshipped many gods, probably adding to them as traders of different tribes arrived in the city, and there were more than 350 idols in the Ka'bah. The gods worshipped by the people of Makkah included Allah (the word means 'the god') but among the other gods were Allat, the wife of Allah, and the three daughters of Allah: al-Lat (the Sun), al-Uzza (Venus, the planet), and Manat (Fate, good fortune or Lady Luck).

Muhammad ﷺ was born into the Hashemite clan of the ruling tribe of Makkah, the Quraish, but he had a sad childhood. His father, Abdullah, died before Muhammad ﷺ was born, and his mother, Amina, died when he was six. He was put in the care of his grandfather, but when his grandfather died two years later, Muhammad ﷺ was looked after by his uncle, Abu Talib.

When he grew up, Muhammad ﷺ became a trader and his honesty earned him the name of al-Amin, the trustworthy one. He worked for a rich widow, Khadijah, and eventually they married. Khadijah was older than Muhammad ﷺ but it was a successful, happy marriage and they had six children.

Muhammad ﷺ felt that life in Makkah was not how it should be in a holy city. The people made a great show of worshipping their many idols and offering animal sacrifices before they ate their meat, but the rich treated the poor very badly, there was much drunkenness, lying and cheating, and the only thing most people seemed to care about was money. Muhammad ﷺ often spent time in prayer and fasting. He was interested in the monotheistic ideas of the Jews and Christians he met, and of the Hanifs, who were Arab thinkers also disillusioned with polytheism.

REVELATIONS

Muhammad ﷺ was called to be a prophet in 611 CE when he was forty. He had a very strange religious experience when he was meditating in a cave on Mount Nur in the ninth month, Ramadan. The occasion is now known as *Laylat-ul-Qadr*, the Night of Power. The Prophet saw this amazing figure astride the horizon and, wherever he looked, the figure was still there. It was the angel Jibril (Gabriel) and the angel ordered the terrified man to read. Muhammad ﷺ tried to explain that he was illiterate; he could not read. Three times Jibril made his command and three times Muhammad ﷺ gave his reply, but it felt as if the words were burning inside him. Jibril continued to speak and Muhammad ﷺ found himself repeating these words after him:

> *Proclaim! In the name of thy Lord and Cherisher, Who created — Created man, out of (mere) clot of blood. Proclaim! And thy Lord is Most Bountiful — He Who taught (the use of) the pen — Taught man that which he knew not.*
>
> (Surah 96:2–5)

The angel then said, *'O Muhammad you are the messenger of Allah and I am Jibril,'* and departed.

Muhammad ﷺ ran home, convinced that he was going mad, but Khadijah believed that his experience was true and she comforted him. She took him to her Christian cousin, Waraqa, who confirmed that

The cave on Mount Nur where Jibril spoke to Muhammad ﷺ

Muhammad ﷺ was the prophet to the Arabs which the Christian Bible had foretold.

Muhammad ﷺ received his second revelation, Surah 74 (The One Wrapped Up), whilst at home resting, using a cloak as a blanket. The revelation ordered him to rise and warn the people of Makkah.

The first followers of his message, besides Khadijah, were his cousin 'Ali, his friend Abu Bakr and a slave he had freed called Zayd Bin Haritha. The small group began to hold prayers in which they prostrated themselves facing Jerusalem in submission to Allah.

PERSECUTION

In 613 CE Muhammad ﷺ began to preach more publicly. The people of Makkah rejected his teachings. They did not appreciate his criticisms of their idolatry and their behaviour and they feared that his ideas might damage their trade as much of their wealth came from pilgrims visiting the city.

The hostility soon became open persecution. There were attempts on the Prophet's life and some of his followers were tortured and even killed. Persecution became so bad that Muhammad ﷺ sent 83 Muslims and their dependants to Abyssinia (now Ethiopia) because their clans were rejecting them.

The Prophet and his family were protected by his uncle, Abu Talib, even though he never became a Muslim.

Muhammad ﷺ continued to be visited by Jibril. One night Jibril brought a creature for him to ride. Its name was Buraq and, according to some accounts, it had the face of a woman, the body of a mule and the tail of a peacock and it rode like the wind. Buraq took Muhammad ﷺ on a night journey to al-Quds (Jerusalem). There, Muhammad ﷺ climbed a ladder to the seven heavens, met the great prophets of the past and then came to the very throne of Allah. It was during this revelation, which is called the Mi'raj, that Muhammad ﷺ received the instructions that there should be five prayer times each day.

Soon after the night journey some converts from the town of Yathrib, an oasis three hundred miles to the north, brought others from their town to hear the prophet. The inhabitants of Yathrib were experiencing a time of transition. They were building up their trade and a power struggle was developing between various alliances of Jewish and Arab clans. In 622 CE a delegation came from Yathrib to ask Muhammad ﷺ to come to their city not only as their prophet but also as their political leader to unite the various factions.

Persecution in Makkah had become so bad that Muhammad ﷺ was not even allowed to preach. Going to Yathrib would give him the opportunity to organise a community based on Islam, submission to Allah. Seventy followers went on ahead to Yathrib. The name of the city became al-Madinah an-Nabi – the city of the Prophet. Now it is known simply as al-Madinah, the City.

There are many stories of the adventures of Muhammad ﷺ and his companions as they left Makkah. Legend has it that Muhammad ﷺ hid in a cave when he was being pursued but his enemies passed by because they thought the cave must be unoccupied when they saw that a spider had spun a web across the entrance and a dove had built its nest there.

This event is know as the 'migration' and it was so significant an event that al-Hijra, the exit, the departure, of Muhammad ﷺ and his followers from Makkah to al-Madinah in 622 CE marks the beginning of the Muslim calendar, the year 1 AH (Anno Hegirae)

POLITICS AND WARS

A song was composed by people of al-Madinah when Muhammad ﷺ first arrived there from Makkah:

> *The full moon has arrived and grace is upon us, the messenger is with us. He came in accordance with God's order, welcome the best of messengers to al-Madinah.*

Politics in Arabia at the time were based on tribes and clans. Tribal society had many codes of honour and the people were very brave and hospitable; but they were also superstitious. Some of their practices would seem to us to be barbaric; for example, male children were regarded as a blessing but female babies were often killed. Also, blood feuds between clans could never end without loss of life or loss of honour. Alliances between clans had turned blood feuds in al-Madinah into a civil war. Both sides accepted the arbitration of Muhammad ﷺ who based the laws of his new community not on the politics of tribalism but on religion. It was to be a theocracy ruled by God. At first, he was supported by the Jewish clans because they believed in one God and an ethical code based on religion, but arguments broke out because Muhammad ﷺ regarded Jesus as a prophet. Revelations of the Qur'an which were received during this time resulted in changes such as the qiblah (direction for prayer) becoming the Ka'bah in Makkah, not Jerusalem.

The Prophet's mosque in al-Madinah

Establishing the new state was not easy. There were armed conflicts between the clans of al-Madinah and constant threats from Makkah. Muhammad ﷺ made rules to help widows and orphans, of which there were many because of the fighting, and demonstrated the skills of a true statesman in organising the life of the new community. Life at al-Madinah was the beginning of the Ummah which is now the worldwide Muslim community.

The Battle of Badr in 624 CE is an important event to Muslims. Muhammad ﷺ led his followers into battle to defend the safety of the Muslims in al-Madinah against Makkan violence. This battle confirmed the military, political and religious leadership of the Prophet, and as a result of this success, his authority was accepted in al-Madinah. All the Arab clans officially became Muslims, and so did some Jews though others left al-Madinah. Some Jews retained their own religion and stayed. They were protected and not persecuted, but their rights were restricted.

Skirmishes with Makkah continued and then, in 625 CE, 3,000 Makkans marched on al-Madinah. The Battle of Uhud was technically a Makkan victory but the Makkans did not take advantage of this and Muhammad ﷺ was left in control of the trade route. It was two years before the Makkans tried again.

In 627 CE 10,000 Makkans marched on al-Madinah. This is called the Battle of al-Khandaq (the Trench) because, before the enemy arrived, the crops were harvested and a huge trench was dug with stakes in it. This caused confusion and the eventual retreat of the Makkan cavalry.

A treaty was made between Makkah and al-Madinah at Hudaybiya, north of Makkah, in 628 CE. Muhammad ﷺ was in a very strong position by then but he did not make excessive demands. His main concern was for Muslims from al-Madinah to be able to make the pilgrimage to the sacred Ka'bah shrine unmolested.

In 629 CE Muhammad ﷺ led the pilgrimage to Makkah. It had a great effect on public opinion in the city. They saw they had nothing to fear from Islam, so when a Makkan force broke the treaty in 630 CE and attacked a tribe under the protection of Muhammad ﷺ, there were many people in Makkah who sympathised with the Muslims. Muhammad ﷺ camped outside Makkah and sent a warning that everyone should stay indoors when his army entered the city and they would not be hurt. Many stayed indoors. There was some fighting but Makkah surrendered to the army of Muhammad ﷺ.

When he entered Makkah, the Prophet went straight to the Ka'bah, rode round it seven times and then cleansed it by destroying all the idols.

THE LAST SERMON

Muhammad ﷺ died in al-Madinah in 632 CE. During his life, his main task had been to be the messenger chosen to recite the revelation of the Qur'an. He was also the source of many sayings, hadith, which are found in authenticated collections. They are not as important as the Qur'an but they provide an example for Muslims to follow in their daily lives.

A fitting conclusion to any account of the life of the Prophet is the last sermon which he preached on Mount Arafat at the end of the Hajj:

O people, listen to my words carefully, for I know not whether I would meet you again on such an occasion.

O people, just as you regard this month, this day, this city as sacred, so regard the life and property of every Muslim as a sacred trust. Remember that you will indeed appear before Allah and answer for your actions.

Return the things kept with you as a trust to their rightful owners. All dues of interest shall stand cancelled and you will have only your capital back; Allah has forbidden interest, and I cancel the dues of interest payable to my uncle 'Abbas bin 'Abdul Muttalib.

O people, your wives have a certain right over you and you have certain rights over them. Treat them well and be kind to them, for they are your partners and committed helpers. Beware of Satan, he is desperate to divert you from the worship of Allah, so beware of him in matters of your religion.

O people, listen carefully! All the believers are brothers. You are not allowed to take things belonging to another Muslim unless he gives it to you willingly.

The place of the last sermon at Arafat

O people, none is higher than the other unless he is higher in obedience to Allah. No Arab is superior to a non-Arab except in piety.

O people, reflect on my words. I leave behind me two things, the Qur'an and my example, and if you follow these, you will not fail.

Listen to me carefully! Worship Allah and offer Salah, observe Sawm in the month of Ramadan and pay Zakah.

O people, be mindful of those who work under you. Feed and clothe them as you feed and clothe yourselves.

O people, no prophet or messenger will come after me and no new faith will emerge.

All those who listen to me shall pass on my words to others, and those to others again.

(Hadith)

THE PRACTICE OF THE FIVE PILLARS

As part of their submission to the Will of Allah, Muslims follow the Five Pillars which are visible signs of their way of life and the unity of the *Ummah*, the worldwide Muslim community:

- **Shahadah** (Declaration of faith) – 'There is no god but Allah; Muhammad is the messenger of Allah'

- **Salah** (Compulsory prayers five times a day):
  - *Fajr* (between dawn and sunrise)
  - *Zuhr* (after mid-day)
  - *'Asr* (between late afternoon and sunset)
  - *Maghrib* (between sunset and the end of daylight)
  - *'Isha'* (night, until dawn).
- **Zakah** (Purification of wealth by payment of annual welfare due) – usually $2\frac{1}{2}$% of surplus income given annually. Zakah began in al-Madinah when there were widows and orphans to be looked after. Muslims regard wealth as a gift from Allah for the benefit of humanity and it should be shared. It is a sign of brotherhood and unity. It also benefits the givers in that it frees them from greed, selfishness, materialism and hypocrisy. It helps their spiritual growth, so zakah is often linked with salah.
- **Hajj** (Pilgrimage to Makkah) made during the month of Dhul-Hijjah. This duty must be observed once in a lifetime by all Muslims who are physically and mentally able to do so and who have sufficient funds to take care of their dependants whilst they are away from home.
- **Sawm** (Fasting in the month of Ramadan – during the hours of daylight.) The month of fasting is a time of testing oneself to the limits. It is a time of prayer and good deeds. It is the time when the Qur'an was first revealed to the prophet Muhammad ﷺ and it is the month when Allah looks down with special favour on humanity.

These Five Pillars are said to support the faith of Islam as pillars support a house. They are important individually but also as a whole.

THE FIVE PILLARS

SHAHADAH | SALAH | ZAKAH | SAWM | HAJJ

FOR DISCUSSION

Consider how observing the Five Pillars might influence the life of a Muslim today. Make sure that you look at the positive effects of living a religious life as well as any negative ones.

JIHAD

The most excellent man is one who works hard in the way of Allah with his life and property.

The best Jihad is to speak the truth before a tyrant ruler.

(Hadith)

Jihad was ordained at al-Madinah in the second year of Hijrah. Jihad is the word used for the personal struggle of every Muslim to follow the teachings of Islam and to resist evil. It literally means 'striving' or 'trying the best you possibly can'. Sometimes this includes a physical battle against enemies of Islam and the willingness to accept martyrdom as the ultimate submission to Allah. It is important when studying Islam, however, to realise that physical fighting is not the main meaning of Jihad. Most of all, Jihad is a lifestyle following the example of Muhammad ﷺ in good conduct and in the struggle against evil. The aim of Jihad is to establish the Islamic system of life in order to fulfil the will of Allah and gain Allah's favour.

The word Islam is related to the word for peace and Islam is a peace-loving religion. However, even the most peaceful people sometimes find themselves in situations which involve conflict. Muslims are not pacifists, but they believe that all ways of solving disputes should be tried before resorting to physical violence. Muhammad ﷺ taught that Muslims must defend Islam and he led his followers into battle. Islam is a practical religion and there are rules to be considered about the reasons for going to war and the way the conflict will be conducted to ensure that a war is acceptable to Allah.

A war is **not** Jihad if:

- War is declared by a political leader rather than a religious leader.
- An individual declares war without the support of the Muslim community.
- The war is aggressive not defensive.
- The purpose is to gain land or power.

FOR DISCUSSION

Sometimes Jihad is described as being a sixth pillar of Islam but some Muslims do not like this description. Can you suggest reasons for both points of view?

- The purpose is to force conversion to Islam.
- Peaceful alternative ways of solving the problem have not been tried.
- Innocent women and children are exposed to physical danger.
- Trees, crops and animals have not been protected.

If two parties among the Believers fall into a quarrel, make ye peace between them: but if one of them transgresses beyond bounds against the other, then fight ye (all) against the one that transgresses until it complies with the command of Allah; but if it complies, then make peace between them with justice, and be fair: for Allah loves those who are fair (and just).

(Surah 49:9)

To those against whom war is made, permission is given (to fight), because they are wronged – and verily, Allah is Most Powerful for their aid – (They are) those who have been expelled from their homes in defiance of right – (for no cause) except that they say, 'Our Lord is Allah'. Did not Allah check one set of people by means of another there would surely have been pulled down monasteries, churches, synagogues, and mosques, in which the name of Allah is commemorated in abundant measure. Allah will certainly aid those who aid His (cause) – for verily Allah is Full of Strength, Exalted in Might, (Able to enforce His Will).

(Surah 22:39–40)

FOR DISCUSSION

Muslims believe that people are Allah's *khalifahs* (deputies) on earth. How might being a good khalifah overlap with Jihad?

PRACTICE EXAMINATION QUESTIONS

1 (a) **What do Muslims believe about God?**
    (*8 marks*)

    You are being asked to outline Muslim beliefs about God. The key fact is that Muslims are monotheistic; the Qur'an says there is one God and only one God. The word for God is Allah. Allah is the one, compassionate, creator God and all other beliefs follow from that e.g. about His power and His nature.

   (b) **Explain the importance of Muhammad ﷺ for Muslims.** (*7 marks*)

    It is necessary to explain that Muhammad ﷺ is not worshipped by Muslims and to make clear his status as the final prophet and reciter of the revelation of the Qur'an. Credit will be given for other aspects of his importance such as the fact that he is an example for Muslims.

   (c) **'Prayer is the most important of the Five Pillars for Muslims.'**

    Do you agree? Give reasons to support your answer and show that you have thought about different points of view. (*5 marks*)

    Notice that the argument is not just about the importance of prayer but about whether or not it is the most important of the Five Pillars for Muslims. You may suggest other pillars as more important or you may wish to argue that all are important but you must consider arguments for different points of view. Arguments are expected to be based on sound knowledge and understanding of Muslim attitudes.

2 (a) **Give an account of how Muhammad ﷺ was called to be the Prophet of Islam.** (*8 marks*)

    An account of the appearance of the angel Jibril on Mount Nur commanding Muhammad ﷺ to recite is the main part of the answer but it needs to be set in the general background of the time, place and situation in which the Prophet lived.

   (b) **Explain what was special about the message of Muhammad ﷺ.** (*7 marks*)

    That an angel delivered it may demonstrate that the message was special but the explanation should include the content of the message of the Qur'an about the need for people to worship Allah rather than idols and the inevitability of judgement if they refuse to follow the straight path. The continuity with the past messages is relevant as is the contrast with beliefs of his contemporaries, though the latter is not essential. The message of Muhammad ﷺ was also significant because of its nature. It was not the words of Muhammad ﷺ, it is the words of Allah. It is a revelation.

   (c) **'It is difficult for a Muslim in the twenty-first century to follow the example of Muhammad ﷺ'.**

    Do you agree? Give reasons to support your answer and show that you have thought about different points of view. (*5 marks*)

    You may agree or disagree but remember to include arguments in support of your view and to consider the reasons why other people may disagree with your view. You may wish to discuss certain parts of the quotation in particular. For example you may think that it is difficult but not impossible and that the century is not significant in following a religion and a book which have existed such a long time.

3 (a) What do Muslims believe will happen after they die? (*8 marks*)

Include as many details as you can about Muslim beliefs about immediately after death (see Chapter 6) and about the afterlife but do remember that Muslims do not believe in reincarnation.

(b) Explain why Jihad is important for Muslims. (*7 marks*)

The important thing to explain about Jihad is that it is not only about physical fighting. Islam is a complete way of life. Muslims should show their convictions in their daily lives. This struggle against evil may be shown in many different ways and any sensible examples will be given credit.

(c) 'Religion is about peace and justice so believers should never fight anybody.'
Do you agree? Give reasons to support your answer and show that you have thought about other points of view. You must refer to Islam in your answer. (*5 marks*)

Remember that you should refer to Islam in some part of your answer. Arguments should be based on sound knowledge and understanding so it is likely that you will refer to the fact that Islam is not a pacifist religion but that Jihad is not necessarily about physical violence. This is a structured question and you may find yourself referring back to points you made in earlier parts of the question.

THE MUSLIM DECLARATION ON NATURE
His Excellency Dr Abdullah Omar Nasseef
Secretary General, Muslim World League

THE ESSENCE OF Islamic teaching is that the entire universe is God's creation. Allah makes the waters flow upon the earth, upholds the heavens, makes the rain fall and keeps the boundaries between day and night. The whole of the rich and wonderful universe belongs to God, its maker. It is God who created the plants and the animals in their pairs and gave them the means to multiply. Then God created mankind – a very special creation because mankind alone was created with reason and the power to think and even the means to turn against his Creator. Mankind has the potential to acquire a status higher than that of the angels or sink lower than the lowliest of the beasts.

The world 'Islam' has the dual meaning of submission and peace. Mankind is special, a very particular creation of Allah. But still we are God's creation and we can only properly understand ourselves when we recognise that our proper condition is one of submission to the God who made us. And only when we submit to the Will of God can we find peace: peace within us as individuals, peace between man and man, and peace between man and nature. When we submit to the Will of God, we become aware of the sublime fact that all our powers, potentials, skills and knowledge are granted to us by God. We are His servants and when we are conscious of that, when we realise that all our achievements derive from the Mercy of God, when we return proper thanks and respect and worship to God for our nature and creation, then we become free. Our freedom is that of being sensible, aware, responsible trustees of God's gifts and bounty.

For the Muslim, mankind's role on earth is that of a *khalifa*, viceregent or trustee of God. We are God's stewards and agents on Earth. We are not masters of this Earth; it does not belong to us to do what we wish. It belongs to God and He has entrusted us with its safekeeping. Our function as viceregents, *Khalifa* of God, is only to oversee the trust. The *khalifa* is answerable for his/her actions, for the way in which he/she uses or abuses the trust of God.

Islam teaches us that we have been created by God and that we will return to god for Judgement; that we are accountable for our deeds as well as our omissions. The *khalifa* will render an account of how he treated the trust of God on the Day of Reckoning. The notion that describes the accountability of the *khalifa* is *akhrah*. Islam is the guidance of how to live today so that we can face the *akhrah*; it is the Message which informs us of what will be involved in that reckoning.

The central concept of Islam is *tawheed* or the Unity of god. Allah is Unity; and His Unity is also reflected in the unity of mankind, and the unity of man and nature. His trustees are responsible for maintaining the unit of His creation, the integrity of the Earth, its flora and fauna, its wildlife and natural environment. Unity cannot be had by discord, by setting one need against another or letting one end predominate over another; it is maintained by balance and harmony. Therefore Muslims say that Islam is the middle path and we will be answerable for how we have walked this path, how we have maintained balance and harmony in the whole of creation around us.

So unity, trusteeship and accountability, that is *tawheed*, *khalifa* and *akhrah*, the three central concepts of Islam, are also the pillars of the environmental ethics of Islam. They constitute the basic values taught by the Qur'an. It is these values which led Muhammad, the Prophet of Islam, to say: 'Whoever plants a tree and diligently looks after it until it matures and bears fruit is rewarded', and 'If a Muslim plants a tree or sows a field and men and beasts and birds eat from it, all of it is charity on his part', and again, 'The world is green and beautiful and God has appointed you his stewards over it.' Environmental consciousness is born when such values are adopted and become an intrinsic part of our mental and physical makeup.

And these are not remote, other-worldly, notions; they concern us here and now. If you were to ask me what the notion of the Hereafter has to do with here and now, my answer might surprise you. I would say nuclear power and biotechnology. Both of these are very present here-and-now issues. Both have benefits and costs. Both have implications for the health and well being of mankind and nature. If I sincerely intend to be God's *khalifa*, His steward on Earth, then I must have an opinion about them, must prepare myself to make choices about them, because I will be accountable for what mankind has wrought with these devices in the Hereafter.

Islam is a very practical world-view. It seeks, in all is principles and injunctions, to give pragmatic shapes to its concepts and values. Indeed, the notions of *tawheed* and *khalifa* have been translated into practical injunctions in the *Shariah*. Such *Shariah* institutions as *haram* zones, inviolate areas within which development is prohibited to protect natural resources, and *hima*, reserves established solely for the conservation of wildlife and forests, form the core of the environmental legislation of Islam. The Classical Muslim jurist, Izz ad-Din ibn Abd as-Salam, used these aspects of the *Shariah* when he formulated the bill of legal rights of animals in the thirteenth century. Similarly, numerous other jurists and scholars developed legislations to safeguard water resources, prevent over-grazing, conserve forests, limit the growth of cities, protect cultural property and so on. Islam's environmental ethics then are not limited to metaphysical notions; it provides a practical guide as well.

Muslims need to return to this nexus of values, this way of understanding themselves and their environment. The notions of unity, trusteeship and accountability should not be reduced to matters of personal piety; they must guide all aspects of their life and work. *Shariah* should not be relegated just to issues of crime and punishment, it must also become the vanguard for environmental legislation. We often say that Islam is a complete way of life, by which it is meant that our ethical system provides the bearings for all our actions. Yet our actions often undermine the very values we cherish. Often while working as scientists or technologists, economists or politicians, we act contrary to the environmental dictates of Islam. We must imbibe these values into our very being. We must judge our actions by them. They furnish us with a world-view which enables us to ask environmentally appropriate questions, draw up the right balance sheet of possibilities, properly weigh the environmental costs and benefits of what we want, what we can do within the ethical boundaries established by God, without violating the rights of His other creations. If we use the same values, the same understanding in our work as scientists or technologists, economists or politicians as we do to know ourselves as Muslims – those who submit themselves to the Will of God – then, I believe, we will create a true Islamic alternative, a caring and practical way of being, doing and knowing, to the environmentally destructive thought and action which dominates the world today.

2

FESTIVALS, FASTS AND SPECIAL DAYS

The ways in which Muslims observe:
Ramadan; Id-ul-Fitr and Id-ul-Adha; Salat-ul-Jumu'ah prayers on Friday.
The significance of these times for Muslims.

Most religions have days and times of year that are special, or sacred.

Having a regular cycle of events to plan, look forward to and experience together strengthens community spirit, and the celebrations remind believers of past events in their religion and the beliefs they have in common.

When studying Islam, it is important to understand that Muslims follow a lunar calendar, measured by the moon. A new month begins with a new moon. The year has twelve lunar months of twenty-nine or thirty days. A new day begins in the evening with the appearance of the moon.

The months of the Muslim year

Muharram	
Safar	
Rabi al-Awwal	
Rabi al-Akhir	
Jumada al-Ula	
Jumada al-Akrah	
Rajab	
Shabaan	
Ramadan	the month of fasting
Shawwal	Id ul-Fitr is on the first of Shawwal
Dhul Qidah	
Dhul Hijjah	Id ul-Adha begins on the tenth of Dhul Hijjah

The Muslim year contains 354 days. As the lunar year is shorter by ten or eleven days than the solar year (measured by the sun) the lunar months are not fixed to the seasons but gradually move through them.

ICT FOR RESEARCH

Download a copy of the Muslim calendar for the current year:
www.assirat.org

RAMADAN

Ramadan is a special time for Muslims. It is not just a special day, nor a few days; it is a whole month.

Ramadan is the month when Muslims observe *Sawm*, Fasting, which is one of the Five Pillars of Islam.

FOR DISCUSSION

Have you ever tried to fast or gone without food for some reason? Maybe it was a religious occasion or a sponsored event. Perhaps you had been to see the dentist or you were going into hospital for an operation or you were simply trying to slim. What were your feelings about the experience? How long did the whole thing last? What was the hardest part? What did you miss the most?

HOW MUSLIMS OBSERVE RAMADAN

During the whole month of Ramadan, all healthy adult Muslims should fast during daylight hours. This part of each day is described as during the hours when a white thread can be distinguished from a black thread, or, as the Qur'an expresses it, *'Until the white thread of dawn appear to you distinct from its black thread'* (Surah 2:187).

Fasting in Ramadan does not mean simply giving up sweets or some other enjoyable treat. It means that Muslims should not eat nor drink, nor indulge in pleasures, including sexual activity. They must do nothing sinful and must not think evil thoughts.

The rules of fasting are taken very seriously. Nothing must pass the lips; no food, no drink, no chewing gum and no smoke from cigarettes. Some Muslims even avoid swallowing their own saliva. The self-discipline includes not indulging in idle chatter and certainly not talking about people behind their back. Cleaning teeth and putting drops in the eyes are allowed and so are injections into a muscle. Intravenous nutritional injections are not allowed. Unintentional eating or drinking, such as swallowing water when taking a shower, is excused and it does not invalidate the fast.

Sometimes Ramadan takes place when it is summer and sometimes when it is winter. In Britain, summer days may not always be hot but they are very long and this makes it harder to fast. There are other difficulties which Muslims have to face during Ramadan in non-Muslim countries. Employers may not realise why the Muslim worker is less efficient than usual. Fellow workers may not appreciate the problem and, even if they do understand, they may still resent having to make allowances. The same may apply in school and it can be especially difficult for Muslim students if Ramadan falls at the same time as examinations, sports days or work experience.

A Muslim who deliberately breaks the fast for no good reason must give a meal for 60 people or fast for a further 60 days. There is no point in trying to cheat. Allah sees every action and knows the intention of the heart.

Islam is a compassionate religion and those excused from fasting include children under the age of puberty, women who are menstruating, pregnant or breastfeeding, the aged, the sick, travellers and soldiers. Apart from the elderly and the young, all the others should make up the missing days as soon as possible.

The prayer before breaking the fast is:

O God! For your sake we have fasted and now we break the fast with food you have given us.

Muhammad ﷺ used to break the fast each day with a few dates or a drink and most Muslims follow this sensible tradition of breaking the fast by eating something that is light. This food is called *Iftar*. Dates are particularly favoured because of the *Sunnah*, the example of Muhammad ﷺ, but also because they are regarded as highly nutritious and are symbolic of ancient times; they are the main fruit of Arabia.

Later in the evening, the whole family joins together for a big meal. Muslims are not supposed to eat excessively at this main meal because it would go against the whole idea of the fast. The prayer before the main meal is the *Maghrib*.

FOR DISCUSSION

Can you think of other ways Muslim young people may find it difficult to observe Ramadan at school?

A communal meal during Ramadan

Some city mosques make large evening meals for hundreds of people. In Cairo, there are tables of mercy for poor people who are homeless.

The word *Suhur* is used for the extra meal which is sometimes eaten before daylight when Ramadan falls in long summer days. Salty food is avoided because it makes people thirsty.

Before the fast begins at dawn, a Muslim makes a statement of intention:

> *O God, I intend to fast today in obedience to your command and only to seek your pleasure.*

Obviously it is easier to keep Ramadan in a Muslim country. Banks, businesses, shops, offices and schools close earlier because they have worked through lunchtime. Restaurants, cafés and shops often open after sunset and the atmosphere can be very lively at night.

People sometimes wonder what Muslims do if they live even further north than Britain, in the Arctic, for example, where there are six months of daylight and six months of night. Muslims who live in the Arctic or Antarctic zones are allowed to keep the same length of time as a place nearby which falls outside their zone, or they may simply keep the same number of hours as the Muslims in Makkah.

When studying Ramadan it is easy to concentrate on the rules about what Muslims should not do and the trials and problems associated with fasting. This is especially the case when writing about Muslims in a non-Muslim country such as Britain. There is another side to keeping Ramadan, which should not be forgotten. It is an opportunity not only to give up things but to do positive extra activities which bring a sense of fulfilment and spiritual reward. Muhammad ﷺ himself used to pray hardest in Ramadan according to his wife, especially on the night that was the anniversary of Laylat-ul-Qadr, the Night of Power, when he received the first revelation from the angel Jibril. The exact date is not certain but it is thought to be the 27th of Ramadan when:

A Muslim family breaking their fast

We sent down the (Qur'an) in Truth, and in Truth has it descended
(Surah 17:105).

Many Muslims make a point of reading the whole Qur'an in this month and the 114 surahs are divided into thirty equal sections to help them do this. Some may stay up all night reciting on the 27th of the month.

In the North of England there is a radio station, Fast FM, which broadcasts for this one month each year. It tells Muslims the exact times each day for starting and finishing the fast and it features programmes of readings of the Qur'an. National television also presents programmes about Muslim practices, too, and this is seen as an opportunity for Muslims to tell other people about Allah.

In the month of Ramadan Muslims use the time saved from more frivolous pursuits to help the poor and to pray more, especially *Du'a* (personal, optional) prayers. Besides the usual five daily prayers there is an additional salah called *Tarawih*, which is performed after the 'Isha' prayer. The last ten days of Ramadan are particularly associated with worship and prayer at the mosque. Many Muslims learn over the years to look forward to this annual opportunity to take life more seriously and to grow more devout in their faith and practice.

THE SIGNIFICANCE OF RAMADAN FOR MUSLIMS

> *O ye who believe! Fasting is prescribed to you as it was prescribed to those before you, that ye may (learn) self restraint*
>
> (Surah 2:183).

Many religions practise fasting. For some, the denial of bodily appetites is part of a strict and severe attitude to life. This is not the case in Islam. Muslims love life because every day is full of blessings from Allah. The discipline of observing the fast is meant to help Muslims appreciate everything that Allah has given them.

One reason why Muslims fast is that doing so is an act of obedience. It is their duty to fast in Ramadan because Sawm is one of the Five Pillars they must keep. The Qur'an, the word of Allah, commands them to fast and Muhammad ﷺ set the example. Sawm is meant to be an act of 'ibadah (obedience), but there is more to it than simply doing what you are told because you are forced or feel you are obliged to do so. Muslims should keep the duty gladly, not resentfully, because obedience is part of submission and worship. As in all Muslim practices, the intention is important as well as the action. So, an act of 'ibadah is an act of sincere obedience, submission and worship.

In the quotation from Surah 2 above, there is a reference to the fact that fasting was prescribed for the people who lived before the time of Muhammad ﷺ and his followers. The Jews living in Makkah in those days used to fast on Yom Kippur (the Day of Atonement). When Muhammad ﷺ moved from Makkah to al-Madinah and began establishing the ummah, the sacred community, three of the rules he made as a result of the revelations from Allah were similar to Jewish practices. The Jews were called to their prayers by a ram's horn; they faced Jerusalem when they prayed and they fasted. Muslims believe that people before Muhammad ﷺ had been given the rules of the straight way of living but the rules had become distorted. Muhammad ﷺ, in those early years at al-Madinah, had the people called to prayer by someone known as a *muezzin* (the first muezzin was Bilal, a converted Ethiopian slave), he established Makkah as the direction towards which praying Muslims faced, and he instituted the whole month of Ramadan as the time for fasting.

For Muslims fasting is an act of 'ibadah

IN YOUR NOTES

What other reasons are there for fasting? Start with self restraint or self control and make a list of reasons why people might fast. Look at the statement of intention quoted earlier in this chapter.

Muhammad ﷺ linked the fast with zakah, and this reminds Muslims of another purpose of fasting. Not only will they learn to appreciate the good gifts from Allah which they usually enjoy when they are not fasting, but they will also experience what it is like to be poor and hungry. This will teach them compassion and will result in them being less greedy, less selfish and more charitable towards the needy. Islam emphasises the equality of all believers, and each one of the Five Pillars plays a part in encouraging Muslims to care for others in the ummah, the worldwide community of Islam.

It is not possible to predict all the effects that fasting will have on people who take part. Sometimes the difficulties that Muslims encounter may make them feel disheartened or the temptations may seem excessive in a non-Muslim country when they are surrounded by people eating and advertisements promoting food and drinks; but the stress of these situations may, in fact, prove to be a source of religious development. Struggling against temptation, sharing the experience with other members of the community who are fasting and feeling the support of Allah, may bring great spiritual blessings. Sometimes adult Muslims may find they need to learn again a lesson they learned when they were young. For example, one of the ideas young people first have to explore is that fasting teaches a believer not to be greedy, lazy or selfish in personal and family relationships. As a person grows older they may have to think of the implications of not being greedy, lazy and selfish in terms of the global environment, world issues and lifestyle.

IN YOUR NOTES

Look at the last sermon of Muhammad ﷺ on page 14 and make notes about what he said about the fast.

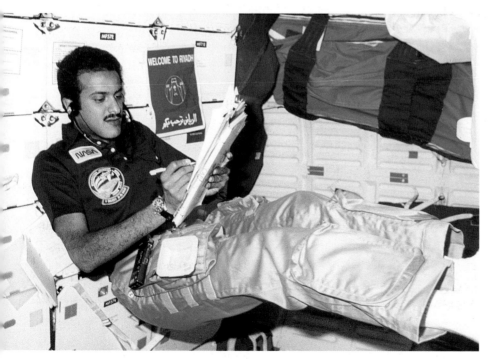

Prince Sultan-bin-Sulman, a member of the Saudi Royal family, was accepted as an astronaut by NASA. The mission was launched during Ramadan. He could have been excused from fasting because he was certainly a traveller. He decided, however, to show his devotion to Allah by fasting in space. Pictures of him were beamed down to earth.

One final reason, to add to the many which might be suggested as to why Muslims fast, is the fact that fasting is rewarded. The first reward is the pleasure of finishing the fast and being able to join in the celebrations at the end of Ramadan with your whole heart and a clear conscience. The second reward will be given at the Day of Judgement.

December 2001 Ramadhan-Shawwal 1422						
S	M	T	W	T	F	S
						1
						15
2	3	4	5	6	7	8
16	17	18	19	20	21	22
9	10	11	12	13	14	15
23	24	25	26	27	28	29
16	17	18	19	20	21	22
1	2	3	4	5	6	7
23	24	25	26	27	28	29
8	9	10	11	12	13	14
30	31					
15	16					

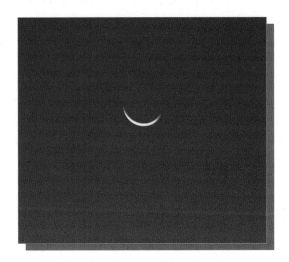

The new moon

Ramadan comes about eleven days earlier each year in relation to the Gregorian calendar.

The end of the month of Ramadan is when the new moon is sighted and it is celebrated with the festival of Id ul-Fitr.

IN YOUR NOTES

Study the following passage from the Qur'an. Think about its meaning and choose a short quotation that you might learn and use in an essay.

(Fasting) for a fixed number of days; but if any of you is ill, or on a journey, the prescribed number (should be made up) from days later. For those who can do it (with hardship), is a ransom, the feeding of one that is indigent. But he that will give more, of his own free will – it is better for him. And it is better for you that ye fast, if ye only knew.

Ramadan is the (month) in which was sent down the Qur'an, as a guide to mankind, also clear (Signs) for guidance and judgement (between right and wrong). So every one of you who is present (at his home) during that month should spend it in fasting, but if anyone is ill, or on a journey, the prescribed period (should be made up) by days later. Allah intends every facility for you; He does not want to put you to difficulties. (He wants you) to complete the prescribed period and to glorify Him in that He has guided you; and perchance ye shall be grateful.

(Surah 2: 184–185)

ID-UL-FITR

In Arabic, the word 'id' means celebration. An *id* is a festival, a feast, a time of happiness.

Id-ul-Fitr is on the first day of the month of Shawwal and it celebrates the successful conclusion of a month of fasting in Ramadan. In Muslim countries it is the start of a three-day holiday.

The Id begins when the new moon appears, signifying the start of the new month. When Muhammad ﷺ lived, people knew the date by keeping watch on the cycles of the moon.

'Id Mubarak'

HOW MUSLIMS OBSERVE ID-UL-FITR

Most people have experienced waiting for an important and exciting event.

Muslim children under twelve do not take part in the fast, and those who are younger may not understand properly what has been happening during Ramadan but they get very excited when Id is coming because decorations are put up, cards are sent and everybody receives presents.

Adults will try to curb their own impatience because they have spent a month not only denying themselves food and drink in the daylight hours but also trying to control their thoughts, desires and emotions. They also, however, are expected to share in the happiness. Muslims are allowed to fast at other times besides the month of Ramadan but they are forbidden to fast during Id-ul-Fitr.

Officially, Ramadan ends and Id begins when the crescent moon is sighted in Makkah. The suspense heightens and the excitement increases as the time draws near for the crescent moon to appear. Nobody knows for sure exactly when the new moon will come. Crowds gather, staring at the sky. Some people climb minarets, skyscrapers and high hills. It is very frustrating on cloudy nights in Britain, especially when Ramadan falls in the winter months.

As soon as the new moon is sighted in Makkah, the information is sent to every mosque and every Saudi Arabian embassy. There is an Id telephone helpline which people can ring in Makkah. Some countries announce it on the radio and television. There may be fireworks or a cannon may be fired as a signal.

All the preparations will have been made. The feasts are waiting but Allah comes first. Before the presents are opened, before the feasting begins, prayers are to be said. Muslims gather together in such large groups that the biggest mosque or the largest place such as a park is used as the community comes together

Id-ul-Fitr is a joyous celebration for Muslims of all ages

Id prayers at the Regent's Park mosque in London

to celebrate the great achievement. Often the service has to be carried out in relays to cope with the large numbers.

There are extra recitations of *'Allahu Akbar'*, 'God is great'. The sermon is usually about responsibility to the poor in the Muslim community. It is the last day for sending *Zakat-ul-Fitr*, which is either actual food or the cost of a meal from each member of the family. In Britain, the local mosque sets the amount that counts as the equivalent of a meal. Muslims in richer countries pay their Zakat-ul-Fitr early so it can be sent in time to the poorer countries. No one should go hungry during Id-ul-Fitr. As individual members of the ummah, Muslims have fulfilled the fast, but as a whole community they join together to share the prayers and celebrations. They greet each other with *'Id Mubarak'* which means 'a happy or blessed Id' and make visits to relatives and friends.

Everybody is wearing his or her best clothes. Presents are exchanged. Prizes are given to younger

Muslims to congratulate them for completing the fast. It may be a new experience and a prize will encourage them to participate in future. Friends and family gather round congratulating each other.

The main meal is at midday. Every country has its own special Id recipes, songs and customs. Some countries have competitions where people recite the Qur'an, whilst others have horse or camel races, village polo matches, acrobats and funfairs. One common tradition is to visit the cemetery.

THE SIGNIFICANCE OF ID-UL-FITR FOR MUSLIMS

The significance of Id-ul-Fitr is clear. It celebrates the successful completion of Ramadan by the individuals and the community. The significance of Ramadan spills over on to Id. Ramadan is one of the Five Pillars. It is compulsory and observing it is regarded as an act of 'ibadah. So there is every reason to celebrate and give presents.

Keeping Id is also itself an act of obedience. Muhammad ﷺ told his followers to observe this festival.

The payment of Zakat-ul-Fitr also illustrates an important point. It shows how the Five Pillars of Islam link together. Muslims are generous because

FOR DISCUSSION

Can you think why Muslims might visit a cemetery at a time of celebration?

they want to thank Allah for his gifts to them and for his strength and help during the difficult time of fasting.

Visiting the graves of the dead at the end of Ramadan is significant because it shows that Ramadan has been a time of contemplating the brevity of this physical life and also shows that Muslims regard the dead as part of the ummah who are to be remembered and included in the celebration. They will rise at the Day of Judgement when all Muslims will receive their reward for keeping Ramadan. However large the crowds might be at Id prayers, Id is a small representation of a much greater celebration at the end of time.

ID-UL-ADHA

Id-ul-Adha is a three-day festival in the 12th month of the Islamic calendar. It begins on the 10th of Dhul-Hijjah and is followed by a further three days of celebration known as *Tashriq* (11–13 Dhul Hijjah). As the months in the Islamic calendar are lunar months based on the cycle of the moon, the festival dates are determined by the sighting of the moon.

Id-ul-Adha is an annual celebration and it comes during the Hajj (the pilgrimage to Makkah). See Chapter 4 on Pilgrimage to learn and understand more about Id-ul-Adha.

HOW MUSLIMS OBSERVE ID-UL-ADHA

Ids are celebrations and therefore many of the ways Muslims observe Id-ul-Adha are the same as the joyful, enthusiastic activities of Id-ul-Fitr. There are prayers, new clothes, feasting and sharing with the poor. What makes Id-ul-Adha special is its links with Hajj.

On the 10th of Dhul-Hijjah, Muslims on Hajj are completing their pilgrimage in an area called Mina where they sacrifice an animal and then change out of the pilgrim clothes they have been wearing. The pilgrims do not celebrate the festival themselves because the timetable of the pilgrimage is too intense.

Animals to be sacrificed at Id-ul-Adha

At home other Muslims show solidarity with the pilgrims and they too offer congregational prayers and sacrifice an animal, according to what they can afford. One family or small community may offer a lamb, a sheep or a goat. Seven families together may offer a cow or a camel. One third of the meat is kept to be eaten by the family and friends while the rest is shared among those who are too poor to purchase an animal.

Islamic law requires animals to be slaughtered in a special way. The animal is turned to face Makkah. The throat is cut by a sharp knife across the jugular vein and prayers are said in the name of Allah. This meat is *halal* (allowed, lawful or permitted) but other meat is *haram* (forbidden). All the blood is drained out. Muslims believe it is unclean to eat the blood of an animal. Only a perfect animal can be sacrificed to Allah.

Muslims are realistic about life. Eating meat involves killing animals. It is the duty of a Muslim man to know how to kill an animal efficiently, quickly and mercifully. In Britain, however, it is the law of the country that animals must be slaughtered at an abattoir by a specially licensed person.

THE SIGNIFICANCE OF ID-UL-ADHA FOR MUSLIMS

Id-ul-Adha is linked with Hajj, one of the Five Pillars. The link with the Pilgrimage is one of the key factors in explaining the significance, importance and meaning of Id-ul-Adha. The festival is a joyful celebration but it also has a serious aspect. It is a time to think about sacrifice.

Allah is generous. He gives many blessings to his followers. He does not expect his followers to deny themselves. Allah wants people to enjoy his gifts but they must not become obsessed with their possessions. Muslims must not put anything or anybody first in their lives before Allah; they must not treat them like gods. That is why at Id-ul-Adha, Muslims commit themselves to being ready to give up everything for God.

Muslims on the Hajj and at home are commemorating the fact that the prophet Ibrahim sacrificed a sheep provided by Allah to take the place of Isma'il, his son. Ibrahim gave a perfect example of this willingness. He was totally obedient to Allah's commands even to the point of being willing to sacrifice his son.

Allah accepted Ibrahim's devotion and obedience and provided a ram to be sacrificed instead.

It is not their meat nor their blood, that reaches Allah: it is your piety that reaches Him.

(Surah 22:37)

During Id, Muslims also remember the farewell sermon (see page 14) which Muhammad ﷺ gave three months before his death. It sums up the principles of the ummah, the Muslim community as laid down in the Qur'anic revelations. Caring for the poor is an important duty. Sharing is an essential part of any celebration in Islam. Id-ul-Adha may be the one time in the year that meat is eaten by some people who are poor, who live in developing countries, or in places hit by war and disasters.

Id-ul-Adha is called the Great Festival. This may be because it is longer than Id-ul-Fitr but it may also be that it is regarded as more important. Both Ids are connected with one of the Five Pillars and both were recommended and observed by Muhammad ﷺ. Islam is a way of life, every part is important and all practices are meant to support the rest.

SALAT-UL-JUMU'AH

Salat ul-Jumu'ah are Friday prayers so this festival takes place once a week.

HOW MUSLIMS OBSERVE SALAT-UL-JUMU'AH

Jumu'ah (Friday) is the Muslim holy day. Friday is *Yaum ul-Juma't*, the Day of Assembly, when Muslims meet at the mosque for midday prayers.

It is not a day of rest. Business may continue as usual on Friday, as there is no religious reason against this (except at the time of prayer). However, in most Muslim countries, the weekend is Thursday and Friday, or Friday and Saturday.

The Friday congregational prayers at the mosque should be attended by every male Muslim who is able to do so. Women are exempt from attending. The prayers are led by the *imam* (leader) who knows the Qur'an and is respected by fellow Muslims. At the start and the end there is a time for optional prayers. The main features are that there is a *khutbah* (sermon) which is read in the language of the community, except for an introduction and conclusion in Arabic, and then the imam leads two *rak'ah fard* (compulsory prayers) instead of the usual four. (See page 72 for the usual pattern of worship in the mosque.) After the prayers there is a time of discussion about topical events.

Prayers at a mosque

THE SIGNIFICANCE OF SALAT-UL-JUMU'AH FOR MUSLIMS

O ye who believe! When the call is proclaimed to prayer on Friday (the Day of Assembly), hasten earnestly to the Remembrance of Allah, and leave off business (and traffic): that is best for you if ye but knew!

(Surah 62:9–10)

The Qur'an states the importance of Salat-ul-Jumu'ah and therefore Muslims accept that Friday prayers are significant. The Qur'an is the word of Allah and Muslims accept its authority and obey what it says. Experience proves that there is wisdom in what the Qur'an says. Meeting regularly as a community is helpful and often there are practical matters to discuss and problems to be solved. Having prayed together there is a sense of unity, co-operation and singleness of purpose. The sermon may have directed people's thoughts towards the celebration of some event, such as the annual festivals, or to some issue which affects the whole of the Ummah (the Islamic worldwide community). Talking together in the mosque afterwards, the men can discuss how this issue might affect the local Muslim community and

the religious principles involved. This opportunity may be very important for Muslim communities, particularly those in non-Muslim countries. Afterwards, Muslims return to their ordinary daily lives. Friday is not a day of rest for them. Religion is part of everyday life, not separate from it.

Muhammad ﷺ is reported to have said:

If a person takes a bath on Friday, washes himself thoroughly, oils his hair, uses such perfume as is available, sets forth for the mosque, does not intrude between two persons, offers the prescribed prayer and listens in silence to the imam, his sins, committed since the previous Friday, are forgiven.

And also:

The sun has neither risen nor set on a better day than Friday. Therein is an hour in which a believing servant praying to Allah for good things finds Allah responding to him.

FOR DISCUSSION

'... it is best for you if you but knew' (Adhan)
Why might prayer be good for people?

PRACTICE EXAMINATION QUESTIONS

1 (a) Describe how Muslims keep Ramadan and state which people are excused. (*8 marks*)

The question as a whole is asking you to think about fasts and festivals. For part (a) you need to describe the way Muslims observe Ramadan and include details of the people who are excused. Check back through this chapter to make sure you know the facts.

(b) Explain why keeping Ramadan and Id-ul-Fitr might strengthen the Muslim community. (*7 marks*)

You are asked to explain why Muslims keep the fast and the festival but the focus is on the way these things help the community. Of course, the religious commitment of individuals might also help the community. If you make your points answer the question, you will be given credit.

(c) 'Religious festivals are more for the benefit of the children than for the adults.'
Do you agree? Give reasons to support your answer and show that you have thought about other points of view. You must refer to Islam in your answer. (*5 marks*)

Finally you are being asked to think back over what you have written. Children are excused from fasting but they join in Id ul-Fitr. Are festivals more for children? Suggest reasons why children enjoy festivals or may benefit from them. Or are festivals more for adults? Think of reasons why adults take part in them. Look back at what you yourself wrote about the reasons for keeping Id ul-Fitr. Of course you may wish to conclude that they are for everybody in the community.

2 (a) Describe the celebrations at Id-ul-Fitr and Id-ul-Adha. (*8 marks*)

For (a) check the descriptions of the two Ids to make sure you have the correct facts. Put in as much detail as possible.

(b) Explain the importance of Salat-ul-Jumu'ah prayers on Fridays. (*7 marks*)

High marks are for explaining the significance of the prayers but of course your answer will make more sense if you take the opportunity to show you know what happens.

(c) 'Regular weekly celebrations are more significant for Muslims than annual festivals.'
Do you agree? Give reasons to support your answer and show that you have thought about other points of view. (*5 marks*)

Finally you are being asked to discuss whether celebrations such as you described in (a) are as significant for Muslims as events which occur more often, such as weekly prayers.

3 (a) **Describe how keeping Ramadan might affect the life of a Muslim in a non-Muslim country.** (*8 marks*)

Look back through the chapter and see how many facts about the keeping of Ramadan could be made relevant to the actual question.

(b) **Explain why Muslim communities in the United Kingdom may find it easier to celebrate Id-ul-Fitr than Id-ul-Adha.** (*7 marks*)

You are asked to show your understanding by making a comparison. You may wish to begin by saying that some things are neither easier nor harder. This would make an explanation of the similarities between the celebrations relevant to the question. The main part of the answer is likely to deal with two aspects: the perceptions of non-Muslims who find Id-ul-Fitr easier to understand and the fact that the sacrifice of an animal has to be dealt with according to the laws of the United Kingdom.

(c) **'Festivals are one of the most important parts of religious life for a Muslim.'**
Do you agree? Give reasons to support your answer and show that you have thought about other points of view. (*5 marks*)

You might decide that there are many parts of Muslim life which are more important than celebrating the two Ids. However, you also need to consider when these take place: at the end of the Hajj and the end of Ramadan which are two of the Five Pillars; also they are opportunities for the community to come together for prayer, for families to celebrate together and for giving zakah. You are being asked how important these festivals are and so you need to produce a balanced argument, perhaps comparing them with other aspects of religious life.

3

MAJOR DIVISIONS AND INTERPRETATIONS

**The main similarities and
differences between Sunni
and Shi'ah Muslims.
How the practice of Islam
might vary in different parts
of the world, e.g. in the
United Kingdom and in a
Muslim state.**

SUNNI AND SHI'AH

There are two main branches of Islam: Sunni Muslims represent
about 90 per cent of the world's Muslim population and Shi'ah
Muslims about 10 per cent. They agree about most beliefs and practices
of Islam.

Shi'ites live mainly in Iran, where it is the state religion, but there
are also many in Iraq and significant minorities of Shi'ah Muslims in the
Arabian Gulf, India, Pakistan, Bangladesh, the Yemen, the Lebanon and
some parts of East Africa.

Numbers of Muslims
per hundred of
population

- 91-100%
- 81-90%
- 51-80%
- 21-50%
- 11-20%
- 5-10%
- 1-4%
- less than 1%

The split between the Sunni and Shi'ah started with an argument about
the succession to the leadership of Muhammad ﷺ and the differences
between the two groups have developed from this dispute.

THE SUNNI – SHI'AH SPLIT

According to tradition, the day that Muhammad ﷺ died was 7th or 8th of June 632 CE. That morning, despite being ill, he had gone to the mosque and the ummah, the Muslim community, were delighted to see him. They thought he must be getting better, but he knew that he was about to die. He reminded them of his teaching and then he said loudly, *'Allah is my witness that you cannot reproach me. Truly, I have allowed what the Qur'an allowed and forbidden what the Qur'an forbade'*.

He returned to the living quarters of his family. During his illness his wives had agreed that he should stay with his youngest wife, A'isha. She was the daughter of Abu Bakr, the closest friend of Muhammad ﷺ. Abu Bakr had been one of the very first converts to Islam and the person whom Muhammad ﷺ had asked to lead the prayers during his illness.

Muhammad ﷺ died at noon with his head in A'isha's lap. Fatimah, the daughter of Khadijah, was also there and so was 'Ali, the husband of Fatimah.

The community was terribly shocked at the death of Muhammad ﷺ and when Abu Bakr heard the news he hurried to A'isha's quarters. From there, he went, weeping, to the mosque and calmed the ummah. The words he said have been remembered ever since. *'If it is Muhammad ﷺ whom you worshipped, he is dead. But if you are servants of Allah, indeed He is the Ever Living One, the Eternal.'*

Muhammad ﷺ had not appointed a successor. The Companions of Muhammad ﷺ asked Abu Bakr to become their leader. He was the first *Khalifah*, which means 'successor', the ruler of the Ummah and the guardian of the *Sunnah* – the tradition based on the life and example of the Prophet Muhammad ﷺ and, hence, the name 'Sunni' Muslims.

Some of the Muslims thought that 'Ali, the cousin and son-in-law of Muhammad ﷺ, should have been the successor. He was still a young man in his early thirties. When he was a little boy of nine or ten, 'Ali was the first male convert to Islam. The Prophet had said of him, *'I am the city of knowledge and 'Ali is its gate.'*

There are many stories of the loyalty of 'Ali. He was the son of Abu Talib, who was the uncle and guardian of Muhammad ﷺ. 'Ali grew up in the household of Muhammad ﷺ so he was more like a younger brother.

It is said that when 'Ali saw the Prophet and his first wife, Khadijah, praying, he was puzzled to see them kneeling in prostration. Muhammad ﷺ explained about the revelations from Allah. 'Ali wanted to accept the message straightaway but felt, as an obedient son, that he should consult his father. The next morning, however, he rushed to tell Muhammad ﷺ, *'Allah created me without consulting my father so why should I consult my father about worshipping Allah?'*

'Ali is also remembered for speaking out at a dinner in front of his older relatives. They were unwilling to help Muhammad ﷺ spread his message and they were unmoved by his testimony. 'Ali said, *'I am the youngest of you. I may be a boy, my feet may not be strong enough, but, O Muhammad ﷺ, I shall be your helper. Whoever opposes you, I shall fight him as a mortal enemy.'*

Later, 'Ali risked his own life as a decoy by pretending to be Muhammad ﷺ so that the Prophet could travel from Makkah to al-Madinah. 'Ali was known as Asadullah, the lion of Allah.

Shi'ah Muslims say that 'Ali was busy arranging the burial of Muhammad ﷺ when the election of Abu Bakr took place.

THE FOUR RIGHTLY-GUIDED KHALIFAHS

During the first thirty years after the death of Muhammad ﷺ the Muslims were governed, in turn, by four Khalifahs who had all been close to the Prophet. They were known as the four *'Rashidin'* (Rightly Guided) Khalifahs.

- **Abu Bakr** 632–634 CE

  He was two years younger than the Prophet and, like Muhammad ﷺ, belonged to the Hashemite clan of the leading Quraysh tribe. There was a danger that the confederation of Arab tribes might split up after the death of the Prophet. Abu Bakr consolidated the position of Islam with a series of skirmishes and battles known as the Ridda (heresy) wars. Abu Bakr was already about sixty when he came to power and he ruled for only two years; then he died. He nominated his successor so there was no election. Ali was passed over once again.

- **'Umar** 634–644 CE

  It was 'Umar who made Muharram the first month of the Muslim calendar to commemorate the *Hijrah*, the departure of Muhammad ﷺ from Makkah to al-Madinah. One of the daughters of 'Umar was Hafsa who preserved many of the recitations of the revelations of the Qur'an.

  'Umar extended the territory of Islam. He took al-Quds (Jerusalem) in 634 CE, Dimashq (Damascus) in 635 CE and al-Iskandariyya (Alexandria) in 642 CE. By the time of his death, the territory had spread as far west as Libya on the North African coast and as far east as Isfahan (Isafan) in Persia (Iraq).

  He was stabbed by Firoz, a Persian Christian, who had a personal grudge about a legal ruling 'Umar had made. Before he died, 'Umar appointed six men to choose the successor. The position was offered to 'Uthman and he was elected.

- **'Uthman** 644–56 CE

  'Uthman was from the Umayyad family of the Quraysh tribe. This family had caused problems for Muhammad ﷺ in Makkah but later converted. 'Uthman had been a faithful companion of Muhammad ﷺ but he is thought to have been a weak Khalifah in that he practised nepotism, showing favoritism to his own tribe and family. He was assassinated whilst at prayer by some Egyptian Muslims. They were revolutionaries who claimed that 'Uthman had not ruled according to the Qur'an and the Sunnah and, therefore, he was an enemy of true Islam.

- **'Ali** 656–661 CE

  Finally, twenty-four years after Muhammad's ﷺ death, 'Ali became Khalifah.

  Shi'ah Muslims, or Shi'ites, are named after the Shi'at of 'Ali, the Party of 'Ali. They refuse to call him the fourth Khalifah because they do not accept the validity of the first three. They call 'Ali the first Imam.

  'Ali's appointment was not wholeheartedly accepted and civil war broke out. The governor of Syria, Mu'awiya, the cousin of 'Uthman, opposed 'Ali and so did A'isha, the widow of Muhammad ﷺ. They criticised 'Ali for not making efforts to track down and punish the murderers of 'Uthman. 'Ali condemned the assassination but he understood why the Egyptians had felt driven to do it.

  'Ali moved his headquarters to al-Kufa in Iraq, and this left his enemies with the opportunity to stir up more opposition in Syria and in the Hijaz (the area around Makkah). There was a series of battles. At the battle of the camel in 657 CE, A'isha was captured but released unharmed and the Battle of Siffin ended in a stalemate because some soldiers put Qur'ans on the ends of their lances and said, *'Let Allah decide'*. Negotiations were made. Peace, or at least a truce, was called but some extremists felt that 'Ali should have continued fighting and Allah would have proved his legitimate authority by helping him to win the battle. 'Ali was assassinated in the mosque at al-Kufa in Iraq in 661 CE, probably by one of the small group of extremists who later became known as the Kharijites (the Seceders). They had already tried to assassinate Mu'awiya but had failed. The Umayyads seized the Khalifate, Mu'awiya declaring himself as 'Ali's successor.

  'Ali's shrine is at Najaf near al-Kufa, which is south-west of Baghdad, in Iraq, though there is some question about where his remains are actually buried. An enormous cemetery has grown up around the shrine and the tombs of some of the other

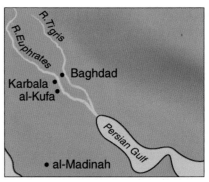

ICT FOR RESEARCH

Use Encarta to find out about another shrine to 'Ali: Mazar-e-Sharif in North Afghanistan.

This mosque at al-Kufa contains the shrine of 'Ali

Imams. The corpses to be buried there are taken inside the shrine then carried three times round the outside of the shrine of 'Ali. Shi'ah Muslims from Iran make pilgrimages to the neighbouring territory of southern Iraq to visit al-Kufa.

One of the sayings of 'Ali was, *'I hold in contempt those who take away the rights of others and I shall make them give back the rights and privileges they have stolen'*.

HASAN AND HUSAYN, THE SONS OF 'ALI

Shi'ah Muslims believe that, after his death, the authority of 'Ali passed to his son Hasan who became their second Imam. The word 'imam' is used differently by Sunni and Shi'ah Muslims. (See page 71 for the role of the imam as the leader of prayers, in the Sunni tradition.) Shi'ah Muslims use 'imam' to mean the divinely appointed leader of their community.

Hasan was forced to renounce any claims to the Khalifate by the powerful Mu'awiya, and retired to al-Madinah where he lived for eight years till his death. It is possible that he was poisoned. Hasan's brother, Husayn, became the third Shi'ah Imam.

Meanwhile, Mu'awiya's son, Yazeed, took over as Khalifah on the death of his father in 679 CE. His succession established the Khalifate as a hereditary system, which continued to rule, from Dimashq in Syria, until 750 CE.

Husayn, 'Ali's son, refused to give his pledge of alliance to Yazeed. During his pilgrimage to Makkah that year, Husayn received a message from some of his supporters in al-Kufa, that they would fight in his defence should he decide to challenge Yazeed and become the rightful Khalifah. After the pilgrimage, Husayn left Makkah and headed for al-Kufa with 72 men and some women and children including his sister, Zainab, and his baby son. Husayn rode his famous horse, Maymun.

Yazeed heard what was happening and gathered an army. There was a confrontation on the 2nd day of Muharram in the year 61 AH (680 CE) near Karbala, twenty-five miles northwest of al-Kufa. One problem for Husayn's followers was that their access to the river was blocked and they began to suffer from lack of water. Some even died of thirst. On the 10th day of the month, the Battle of Karbala took place. It was clear that Husayn's forces had no chance of victory against 4,000 of the enemy, but he chose death rather than compromise. Husayn begged for mercy for his baby son who was in his arms, but the baby was shot with an arrow, which went through his neck and pinned him to his father's arm. Husayn was killed and beheaded. The Umayyad army returned to al-Kufa with the heads of Husayn and his men on their spears. When disrespect was being shown to the head of Husayn, an elderly Muslim made this rebuke, *'I have seen this very face being kissed by the Prophet.'* Sunni Muslims also mourn the death of Husayn, the grandson of Muhammad ﷺ.

Husayn's other son, 'Ali Zayn 'l-'Abidin, was ill at the time of the Karbala battle. He survived and it is from him that the Sayyed, the descendants of the Prophet, come.

Muslims observing the 10th of Muharram

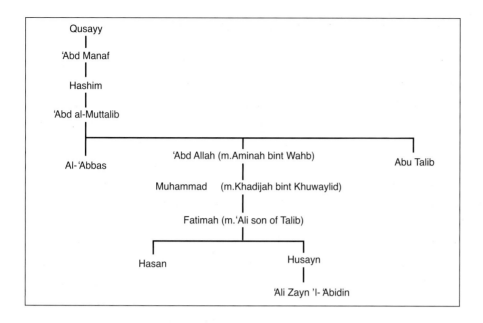

THE 10TH OF MUHARRAM OR ASHURA

The 10th of Muharram was the traditional day of fasting before the time of Muhammad ﷺ. Many Muslims fast on this day and celebrate afterwards because it is traditionally when Noah left the ark after the Flood and when Moses was saved from the Pharaoh. Noah's wife made a special pudding of figs, raisins, dates and nuts, and some Muslims do the same.

For Shi'ah Muslims, however, the 10th of Muharram is especially important. All Shi'ites remember the death of Husayn by mourning during the first ten days of Muharram.

Husayn's shrine at Karbala is the centre of a ten-day festival commemorating his martyrdom. At the end of the festival, a passion play takes place in Kazimayn near Baghdad, which re-enacts the martyrdom, suffering and death of Husayn in battle. In other places, models of his tomb at Karbala are carried in processions.

The celebrations of the festival retell the story as a classic battle between good and evil. Dishes of sherbet are given away to commemorate Husayn's thirst on the battlefield. The processions are accompanied by the singing of dirges and other mournful songs. Men wear black, and women wear black or green. Sometimes a white horse and rider, both smeared with blood or paint, parade through the streets. Some people flagellate themselves with whips or chains and cut their foreheads with razors.

The 10th of Muharram is a very emotional time. Shi'ah Muslims are not only mourning the death of Husayn but committing themselves to be prepared to sacrifice everything for their faith.

Forty days later another play is performed at Husayn's shrine in Karbala. It is called 'the Return of the Head'. When Husayn was killed and beheaded, his head was taken to Yazeed's capital city, Damashq (Damascus) in Syria, but it was returned forty days later and buried with his body in Karbala.

Mu'awiya and his son Yazeem began a Muslim dynasty of Umayyad Khalifahs. This lasted till 750 CE and conquered North Africa and Spain. Arabic remained the language of the religion and culture of Islam. Only the Battle of Poitiers, in France, in 722 CE stopped more of Europe becoming Muslim. The Umayyad dynasty was succeeded by the 'Abbasid Khalifahs.

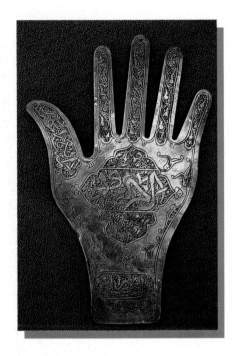

Muhammad ﷺ, Fatimah, 'Ali, Hassan and Husayn are the five key figures in Shi'ah history and theology. They are symbolically represented by a hand print.

THE DIFFERENCES BETWEEN SUNNI MUSLIMS AND SHI'AH MUSLIMS

The difference of opinion about leadership is not simply an argument about who should have led the Muslims centuries ago. The basic issue is whether there should be a family line of rulers, as the supporters of 'Ali maintain, or whether Muhammad ﷺ intended elections to take place to ensure that the most suitable devout person led the ummah. Muslims who held the latter view became known as the Sunni Muslims.

Beliefs about Allah and the practice of the Five Pillars are similar in both groups but there are some differences:

AUTHORITY

Loyalty to the *ahl al bayt* – the house of the Prophet – is at the heart of Shi'ah belief and practice.

Some Shi'ah Muslims include *'Hazrat Ali is the friend of Allah'* in the Declaration of Faith after they have declared their faith in Allah and that Muhammad ﷺ is the prophet of Allah.

Strict Sunni Muslims accuse Shi'ites of showing too much reverence to the family of Muhammad ﷺ whilst Shi'ah Muslims reject the authority of the first four Khalifahs to such an extent that in Iran they celebrate the murder of 'Umar by burning an effigy on a bonfire.

Sunni Muslims accept the authority of the Qur'an as the words of Allah, and of the Sunnah, (the Way of the Prophet), recorded in collections of *hadiths* (see page 105) which can be traced back reliably to Muhammad ﷺ.

Shi'ah Muslims believe that there is secret knowledge hidden in the Qur'an, which was told to 'Ali by Muhammad ﷺ, and that this has been passed down through their Imams. Many hadiths are common to both groups but Shi'ites only accept hadiths which have been transmitted through Shi'ah Muslims. They believe, also, that their Imams had special divine authority, sometimes called a 'guiding light'. The Imams did not sin and could perform miracles. The belief in the authority and inspiration of the Imams makes it difficult for Shi'ah Muslims to accept that Muhammad ﷺ is 'the seal of the prophets' though it remains a key statement of faith. Many also believe that the death of Husayn can bring them salvation from their sins and entry into heaven.

Shi'ah Muslims are divided among themselves about the later Imams and which were the true representatives of Allah. There was a division during the time of the fifth Imam, Muhammad al-Baqir, when the supporters of his half-brother, Zayd, split from the rest of the Shi'ites. There are still followers of Zayd today. They are more moderate in their attitude to the first three Khalifahs whom they accept as well as 'Ali.

The two main branches, however, are divided according to whether they accept seven or twelve Imams. The seveners followed Isma'il as the rightful seventh Imam and they are known as Isma'ilis. Both groups claim their last Imam did not die but disappeared mysteriously and is the Hidden Imam who will return at the end of the world. Some think this returning figure will be the prophet 'Isa (Jesus). The twelfth Imam was Muhammad al-Muntazar. Another name for the Hidden Imam is the Mahdi.

Shi'ites believe that Allah would not leave them without guidance. Their leaders have authority from the Hidden Imam to interpret the Qur'an. Since the disappearance of the Imam (in 873 CE for the twelvers) Shi'ites have been ruled by scholars. The first few were called *babs* (gates) and they were special because they had direct contact with the Hidden Imam rather than contact in dreams.

In Iran, the scholars are called *mujtahids* and their leaders are called *ayatollahs*, which means 'shadows of Allah'. The majority of Shi'ah Muslims in the United Kingdom regard Syed Ali Sistani, who lives in Najaf in Iraq, as their spiritual representative.

Syed Ali Sistani

There is a belief that the Hidden Imam sends a leader to renew and revitalise Shi'ism every century. Ayatollah Khomeini was the renewer for the fifteenth Muslim century.

Other sects have arisen among Shi'ites. The Isma'ili sects include the Druze who claim that a Fatimid Khalifah, al' Hakim, was God, and the Nizari Khojas who are led by the Aga Khan. The Baha'i religion, which started in Iran, also sprang from among the Shi'ites.

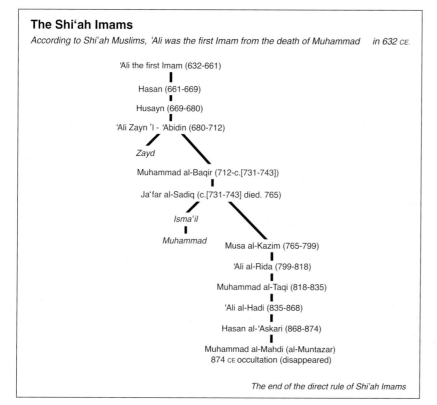

The Shi'ah Imams

According to Shi'ah Muslims, 'Ali was the first Imam from the death of Muhammad in 632 CE.

'Ali the first Imam (632-661)

Hasan (661-669)

Husayn (669-680)

'Ali Zayn 'l - 'Abidin (680-712)

Zayd

Muhammad al-Baqir (712-c.[731-743])

Ja'far al-Sadiq (c.[731-743] died. 765)

Isma'il

Muhammad

Musa al-Kazim (765-799)

'Ali al-Rida (799-818)

Muhammad al-Taqi (818-835)

'Ali al-Hadi (835-868)

Hasan al-'Askari (868-874)

Muhammad al-Mahdi (al-Muntazar)
874 CE occultation (disappeared)

The end of the direct rule of Shi'ah Imams

The Rightly Guided Khalifahs and the twelve Imams

Ayatollah Khomeini led protests against Western influence and against the Shah, the ruler of Iran. The black turban shows that Ayatollah Khomeini claimed descent from Muhammad ﷺ through 'Ali. Ayatollah Khomeini was forced to go into exile for fourteen years. He returned to Iran when the Shah was deposed in 1979, and ruled Iran until his death in 1989.

RELIGIOUS PRACTICES

Shi'ah practices are very similar to Sunni ritual. The differences are not particularly significant.

- The fast at Ramadan is longer for Shi'ites because they wait till the sun has completely set before they close the fast. They also spend three of the days mourning 'Ali because he was martyred on 20 Ramadan.
- Shi'ah Muslims are permitted to pray three times a day instead of five, and washing feet is done at a different part of daily prayers. During prostration, the forehead touches the dust or, preferably, a block of baked mud from Karbala.
- Most Shi'ah Muslims do not regard Friday prayers at the mosque as compulsory though this has changed in Iran since the Islamic Revolution.
- In Sunni countries, zakah (see page 80) is paid to the state, but Shi'ah Muslims pay it to their religious leaders.
- The Shi'ah Muslims have minor pilgrimages, called *ziyara*, to the tombs of the twelve Imams and extra festivals. At Ghadir al-Khumm they celebrate the appointing of 'ali as Imam by Muhammad ﷺ at the pool of Khumm, and they commemorate the martyrdom of Husayn during Muharram. However, Sunni Muslims also show respect towards the Imams and sometimes join in *taziya* (mourning processions).

LAW

Sunni and Shi'ah Muslims accept and interpret the code of Shari'ah law in similar ways. For Shi'ah Muslims, however, the hadith of 'Ali are consulted as well as those of Muhammad ﷺ and, if the issue is still not resolved, the law can be decided by a religious leader who is in contact with the Hidden Imam.

Shi'ah Muslims are not allowed to eat any food prepared by Jews or Christians. They are also allowed to pretend to be either Sunnis or Christians if this will prevent them from being persecuted; the lie will not be a sin. This is called *taqiyya*.

There are a few differences relating to women. Shi'ites accept *muta* (temporary marriage), which could even be for a few hours, to save the honour of the woman and to release the man from committing sin if, for example, a traveller enters into a temporary relationship.

Shi'ah women have more rights of inheritance than Sunni women, usually inheriting equally with the males. Sunni women at best may gain only half of what a male inherits. The strong position of Shi'ah women is because of the importance of Fatimah and Khadijah in the prophet's family. Fatimah, in particular, is regarded very highly among some Shi'ah communities. The Sayyeds claim their descent through Fatimah and so do the Twelve Imams. A'isha and Hafsa are not popular because they are linked with two of the earlier Khalifahs.

POLITICS

Shi'ah Muslims are often portrayed in the West as terrorists and fanatics but their history has forced them to oppose oppressive governments. The argument about the succession was not only about the rights of 'Ali to succeed Muhammad ﷺ but also about the dangers of letting a political dynasty manipulate the situation and take power. It was also about the importance of standing up for religious ideals. All religions have groups who are willing to suffer for the sake of reformation when they feel their religious leaders have forgotten the original teaching.

Western critics sometimes use the word 'fundamentalist' to describe Muslim groups who reject Western secular attitudes and way of life. They are usually referring to terrorist activity and violence done in the name of religion. Many Muslims dislike the use of this term for any group within Islam. The word comes from a Christian context where people also disagree about the meaning. It is used to describe Christians who take the words of their holy book, the Bible, literally but it can also be used to refer to Christians who accept the fundamental truths of the Bible rather than the exact wording. Muslims say that in one sense all Muslims, especially Sunnis, are fundamentalists because they believe the Qur'an contains the actual words of Allah so the term is not appropriate in the context of Islam.

Like many other religions Islam is essentially peace-loving, and it is not the only faith to have some people who feel they have to resort to violence. The name 'Islam' is, however, related to the word for peace. Muslims feel that the media often stereotypes their religion as aggressive and that this is not fair.

Islam is a worldwide living faith. It spread rapidly, not just by the sword as sometimes is claimed, but because it had universal appeal. Trade and cultural factors were part of the story and, probably most important of all, the fact that it is open to all individuals equally regardless of nationality, colour, gender or social status.

Besides the two main groups, the Sunni Muslims and the Shi'ah Muslims, there is one other group which has been important at different times of history, in various areas of the Muslim world, and which influences both Sunni and Shi'ah Muslims. This is the Sufi tradition, which emphasises mystical experience and a relationship with God. Sufis seek purity of the heart rather than putting emphasis on ritual, and they

Fatimah was the youngest daughter of Muhammad ﷺ. She died when she was only thirty. Her outstretched hand is used as a symbol of good fortune and of the blessing and protection of Allah.

FOR DISCUSSION

Muslim countries differ from each other but in all of them the Mu'adhin (muezzin) calls the community to prayer and work stops on Friday for prayers at noon. The Shari'ah Islamic Law is observed and community life reflects Muslim teachings.

- What difficulties might a Muslim in a non-Muslim country, such as the United Kingdom, encounter when trying to be true to his or her faith?
- What positive effects might come from trying to do this?

ICT FOR RESEARCH

Find out how many Muslims there are in China and in Indonesia.

are often in agreement with Shi'ah Muslims against materialism and worldliness.

The largest Sufi order worldwide is the Naqshbandis. Their leader, Shaykh Nazim Adil al-Haqqani, is the fortieth in his line of Khalifahs, which traces its origins to Abu Bakr.

Inevitably, there are variations in the life-styles of Muslim communities around the world. Culture and customs vary and are influenced by history and geography. Life for a Muslim in Iraq will be very different from life for a Muslim in a non-Muslim country such as the United Kingdom.

It is difficult for people of any religion to decide how to apply their faith in a modern world. There are over a million Muslims in the United Kingdom and at least 6 million in the United States of America. Muslims in the West try to separate the essential principles of Islam from customs which are simply cultural traditions. Communities, families and individuals also vary in their beliefs and practice, yet there is an enormous amount of unity in the Ummah.

Chinese Muslims at the Forbidden City in Peking

PRACTICE EXAMINATION QUESTIONS

1 (a) Describe the events which led to the split between Sunni and Shi'ah Muslims. (*8 marks*)

   Description of the events could start with the argument about the succession at the death of Muhammad ﷺ and end with the death of Husayn, but only the main characters and key moments need to be included.

(b) Explain how the lifestyle of Sunni Muslims and Shi'ah Muslims may be similar and different. (*7 marks*)

   The question requires you to show understanding of the fact that the difference of opinion about the succession does not mean that there are enormous differences in the way Sunni and Shi'ah Muslims practise their faith.

(c) 'Differences don't matter; Islam remains the same.'

   Do you agree? Give reasons to support your answer and show that you have thought about other points of view. (*5 marks*)

   Remember to support your opinion with reasons and, when considering other points of view, think what a Sunni or Shi'ah Muslim might say and the arguments they might give.

2 (a) Describe the main differences between Sunni and Shi'ah Muslims. (*8 marks*)

   The main differences stem from the dispute about the succession, so some account of the original split will need to be included.

(b) Explain the difficulties a Muslim might have in practising the Muslim faith in a non-Muslim country. (*8 marks*)

   Some description of the problems which Muslims encounter in a non-Muslim country will be necessary so that your response makes sense, but it is important to make sure you explain why these are difficulties.

(c) 'It is difficult to be a good Muslim in a non-Muslim country.'

   Do you agree? Give reasons to support your answer and show that you have thought about other points of view. (*5 marks*)

   Remember that for each opinion you describe you need to give a reason and you should try to present a balanced argument. As part of the discussion, you may wish to consider what makes a 'good' Muslim.

4

PILGRIMAGE

The nature of pilgrimage in Islam.
The customs and significance of the Hajj.
A consideration of the role pilgrimage might play in the spiritual development of Muslims.

THE NATURE OF PILGRIMAGE IN ISLAM

Most religions have sacred places and when believers go to visit these places we call the believers 'pilgrims' and the journey 'a pilgrimage'.

In some religions pilgrimage is not an important commitment for all believers but in Islam it is essential. The Hajj, the Pilgrimage to Makkah, is one of the Five Pillars of Islam on which the faith rests.

The Hajj takes place annually and it is the duty of every adult Muslim, male or female, who is physically and mentally fit, to make the pilgrimage at least once in a lifetime. The pilgrims must be able to afford the journey without causing hardship to their family back at home.

The Qur'an calls Muslims to *'complete the Hajj or 'Umrah in the service of Allah'* (Surah 2:196). Hajj is the Greater Pilgrimage and can only be taken in Dhul-Hijjah, the 12th month of the lunar calendar; whilst 'Umrah is the Lesser Pilgrimage, which can be taken at any time.

Muslims who live in or near Saudi Arabia can make the journey often and, with modern transport, it is much easier than in the past. Some people, however, live so far away or are so poor that it takes them a lifetime to save for this journey. Sometimes a family or a community collect enough money to send just one person. Borrowing the money is not permitted and, of course, it should not be gained dishonestly or by means which are unacceptable in Islam, such as gambling.

Islam is a compassionate religion and shows consideration towards the sick and the poor. Muslims who are too sick to make the journey can give their Hajj savings to charity or they can pay for a substitute to

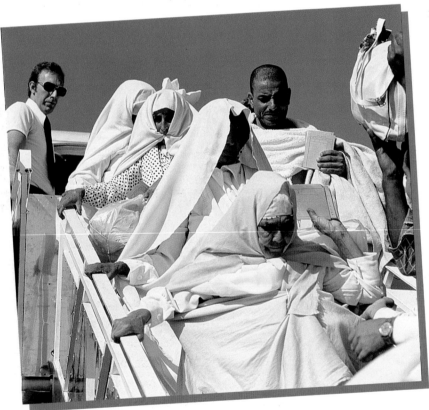

Muslims arriving at Hajj terminal of King Abdul Aziz airport, Jeddah

In the past many pilgrims would have made the journey to Makkah on camels

go to Makkah in their place. The substitute must already have made the pilgrimage on their own behalf.

Those who cannot, for genuine reasons, make the journey have only to declare that it is their *niyyah*, their sincere heartfelt intention, to go on Hajj, and the duty is considered to have been fulfilled. This shows that the importance of the Hajj does not rest merely in doing the physical journey.

The preparations for the Hajj are very important for pilgrims. Planning the journey may involve necessary practical matters such as obtaining a visa from the Saudi Arabian Embassy, booking tickets, accommodation and a guide.

Women who go on Hajj should have a close male relative as their *wakil* or *mahram* (guardian), to protect them. Sometimes groups are organised so that single women may have the protection of an imam or other men from the local Muslim community.

Before setting out, besides making sure they can afford the journey and can provide for the maintenance of their family, pilgrims should pay off all debts and they should make amends for anything they have done wrong.

The most important preparations, however, are those which help the Muslim prepare mentally and spiritually for the pilgrimage. Many pilgrims attend special lessons to learn about the Hajj. The pilgrim must be doing the Hajj for the right reasons. It is for the glory of Allah not for the glory of the person making the journey. Pilgrims must set out wanting to seek God's forgiveness for things they have done wrong in the past and they must be determined, with God's help, to do right in the future.

FOR DISCUSSION

- Where would you like to go at least once in your lifetime?
- What are the differences between pilgrims and tourists?
- When football fans follow their teams to a special match or fans travel to a pop concert, could these journeys be classed as pilgrimages? Give reasons.
- If God is everywhere, why do believers go on pilgrimage?
- What is meant by the term 'sacred places'?
- 'The Hajj is the only one of the Five Pillars which is not compulsory.' How far is this statement true?

The first rite of the pilgrimage is when a Muslim expresses the niyyah, intention, of going on Hajj and puts on the *ihram*: '*Oh God, I intend to perform the Hajj and I am taking Ihram for it. Make it easy for me and accept it from me'*.

The ihram is a white seamless garment similar to the clothes worn by Muhammad ﷺ and the prophets who came before him.

'Putting on ihram' means to enter a state of ritual purity. This involves not only wearing plain white clothing but also avoiding various distractions which might divert the pilgrims from their intention.

Muslims who live in Makkah begin their pilgrimage when they put on ihram.

At certain places called *miqat*, which mark a boundary about ten miles outside the sacred city, the pilgrims travelling to Makkah change from their normal clothes to show they are leaving ordinary life behind. Not even watches or wallets are carried by many pilgrims. This is not the occasion to concentrate on time or money. When they put on ihram, Muslims say two *rakahs* of prayer (see page 76) and ask Allah's help to perform Hajj. Those who travel to Makkah by plane have usually put on ihram before boarding. Usually the pilgrims make *ghusl* (a ritual purifying shower) first. The men may perfume the body, face and beard but not the clothes, and the women should not use perfume at all. After the ghusl, the men also must not use perfume, not even in soap. The men wear two sheets of unsewn white cloth, one round the waist and the other one over the left shoulder. The women wear a long sleeved ankle-length plain garment and, though they cover their heads, their faces are to be left uncovered. This must seem very strange to Muslim women who live in communities where they cover their faces except when they are indoors with their family. Men's heads on Hajj are uncovered but they are allowed to carry an umbrella for shade. Women also may carry umbrellas. Baggage may be carried on top of the head.

Ihram is a symbol of being in a state of spiritual purity

The simplicity of the clothes is not only to guard against vanity but also to emphasise the equality of all of the pilgrims. Allah creates everyone equal and treats everyone equally. A millionaire could be standing next to a humble peasant and nobody should be able to tell the difference. Both would be in similar clothing and would be barefoot or wearing plain simple sandals with toes and heels showing.

Spectacles and hearing aids are allowed and unintentional breaking of the restrictions are excused.

The prohibitions of ihram include:

- no perfume, not even in soap, nor in food,
- no jewellery, except women's wedding rings,
- no wearing of gloves, though hands may be wrapped in cloth,
- no deliberate cutting of hair or fingernails, so as not to interfere with nature,
- no uprooting of plants nor cutting down of trees on the journey,
- no hunting nor bloodshed, except in dealing with bedbugs, fleas, snakes and scorpions,
- no carrying of weapons,
- no sexual relations, not even kissing, nor flirtatious thoughts,
- no engagements nor taking part in weddings.

As servants of Allah, the pilgrims automatically put away everything that may lead to dishonesty, arrogance and aggression. They must also forget the worries and the pleasures of normal life. The pilgrims must be single-minded and not let anything distract them. They should not quarrel nor lose their tempers or be irritable. They are to try to be at peace in their hearts and minds and to accept the hardships of the journey without complaint. During Hajj they are to think of Allah all the time.

From the moment they change into ihram the pilgrims recite the *Talbiyah*, the words they will recite all through Hajj:

Labbayka Allahumma Labbayka – Here I am, O Allah, here I am!

(See page 55 for the Talbiyah in full.)

Read the following excerpt from a pilgrim's account of his preparations and journey:

'... my suitcase was already filled with all the things an aspiring hajj would need ... the two large unsewn strips of terrycloth, the unsewn shoulder sack designed to carry a copy of the Qur'an along with an emergency ration of water, the white umbrella for sun protection, and the broad leather belt to secure the hip cloth, which is worn without anything underneath. The belt is stapled, not sewn together, and offers the customary three inner pockets: one for passport and airline ticket, one for money, and one for medicine because we were only immunised against meningitis. Following the advice of my pilgrim-savvy family physician, I had packed an array of medical articles for the treatment of head and toothaches, stomach disorders, vomiting, diarrhoea, fever, as well as band-aids for bruised and sore feet. I also carried in my suitcase the traditional unsewn sandals...'

Murad Hofmann, 1998

ICT FOR RESEARCH

Visit the web-site of the Ministry of Pilgrimage, Saudi Arabia, to find out the present travel requirements for the pilgrims: www.ummah.org.uk/hajj/travel/ Find out the health requirements for pilgrims to the Hajj this year: www.who.int

FOR DISCUSSION

Non-Muslims are not allowed to visit Makkah. Do you think it is right to stop them? Ask this question again when you reach the end of the chapter.

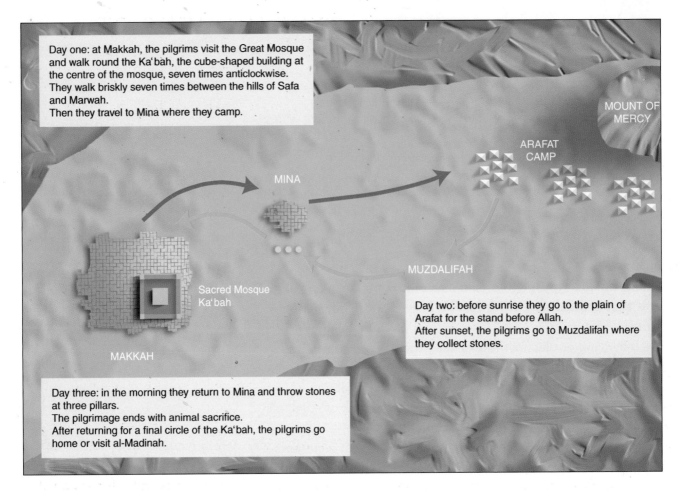

Day one: at Makkah, the pilgrims visit the Great Mosque and walk round the Ka'bah, the cube-shaped building at the centre of the mosque, seven times anticlockwise. They walk briskly seven times between the hills of Safa and Marwah.
Then they travel to Mina where they camp.

MOUNT OF MERCY

ARAFAT CAMP

MINA

MUZDALIFAH

Sacred Mosque Ka'bah

Day two: before sunrise they go to the plain of Arafat for the stand before Allah.
After sunset, the pilgrims go to Muzdalifah where they collect stones.

MAKKAH

Day three: in the morning they return to Mina and throw stones at three pillars.
The pilgrimage ends with animal sacrifice.
After returning for a final circle of the Ka'bah, the pilgrims go home or visit al-Madinah.

The route of the pilgrims

THE CUSTOMS AND SIGNIFICANCE OF HAJJ

The Hajj is probably the largest, most spectacular, gathering of people at any one time and in any one place on earth. It is no wonder that Muslims say that the only greater gathering will be at the Day of Judgement.

Anyone seeing a video or pictures of any part of the Hajj cannot help but be struck by the enormous crowd of people, all dressed the same and all moving towards the same places.

Muhammad ﷺ performed the lesser pilgrimage several times, especially in 629 CE when terms of a treaty with Makkah allowed the Muslims to enter the city for this purpose, but he performed the Hajj only once in his lifetime, in 10 AH, 632 CE, shortly before his death. His example and instructions fixed the details of the route for this holy journey. For fourteen centuries, millions of Muslims from all over the world have made the pilgrimage to the birthplace of Islam.

The Hajj is performed between the 8th and 13th days of Dhul-Hijjah.

There are some variations in the order and ways in which the rites may be performed. These variations go back to the practices of the companions of Muhammad ﷺ and he is recorded as having approved of these actions.

The essential parts of Hajj are the four rites which are obligatory in the Qur'an:

- Putting on ihram
- Doing *tawaf* (circling the Ka'bah)
- Going to Arafat
- Making the last tawaf after returning from Arafat.

ICT FOR RESEARCH

Photographs of places on the route:

http://re-xs.ucsm.ac.uk/re/pilgrimage/route.htm

Though Muhammad ﷺ told his followers they must perform Hajj, the pilgrimage to Makkah began long before his time and Muhammad ﷺ was deliberately re-establishing and purifying an ancient ritual.

To understand the full significance of the Hajj and of the customs essential to the journey, one needs to appreciate the significance of the sacred places which the pilgrims visit.

Places on the pilgrimage are associated with stories about three prophets besides Muhammad ﷺ. These are Adam, Ibrahim and Isma'il (peace be unto them).

ADAM

Adam and Hawwa' (Eve), the first humans created by Allah, had been sent to wander the earth because of their disobedience in al-Jannah (Paradise). They soon became separated from each other and for two hundred years they roamed the earth, lost and unhappy. When they prayed in genuine repentance for forgiveness they were reunited with God and with each other on the 9th of Dhul-Hijjah on the Mount of Mercy, which rises above the Plain of Arafat. The word '*arafat*' means 'recognition'.

Adam is also said to have been the first builder of a shrine on the sacred site where the Ka'bah stands today. As he was being guided to Arafat, he came to the Hijaz, an area where Mecca now stands in Saudi Arabia. He realised he was standing on holy ground, the centre of the world. The angel Jibril (Gabriel) was sent by Allah to tell Adam to build a holy building and Jibril himself provided a shining white stone, the first meteorite that fell to earth, for the corner of the building. After their reunion and forgiveness by Allah on the slopes of Arafat, Adam and Hawwa' were guided by Jibril to perform the Hajj. They spent the night on the Plain of Muzdalifah, then went to Mina and finally on to Makkah where they performed the tawaf by walking round the holy building seven times.

IBRAHIM (ABRAHAM) AND ISMA'IL

Ibrahim, known as *khalil Allah*, the friend of God, is not only an important figure in Islam but also plays a large part in the Jewish and Christian scriptures.

Ibrahim was born about four thousand years ago in Babylon during the reign of King Nimrod. By then people had forgotten Allah. Ibrahim lived in a polytheistic society which believed in many gods and worshipped idols but he believed in the one true God. Ibrahim was persecuted for his beliefs and even thrown into a blazing fire from which, by a miracle, he escaped unharmed.

> *We said, 'O Fire! Be thou cool, and (a means of safety) for Abraham!'* (Surah 21:69)

Life was so difficult for Ibrahim that he and his wife Sarah left Babylon and went first to Palestine, and then to Egypt.

It was in Egypt that Hajar enters the story. The Pharaoh of Egypt tried to seduce the beautiful Sarah and when he was unsuccessful he presented her with a female slave, Hajar, who was probably a captured royal princess taken into slavery.

Sarah and Ibrahim had no children so Sarah suggested, after the custom of the time, that Ibrahim take Hajar as his second wife. Hajar had a son Isma'il and some years later, though she was very old, Sarah miraculously also had a child, Ishaq (Isaac).

As sometimes happens in polygamous marriages, where there is more than one wife, Sarah was jealous of Hajar and especially when Hajar's own son Isma'il was born. She might have harmed them so Ibrahim was told by Allah to take Hajar and her son from Canaan where they lived to a place then called Bakka. There, under a tree, he placed a tent. Nearby stood a mound of earth which was in fact the remains of the ancient shrine built by Adam. The building had been destroyed during the flood at the time of the prophet Nuh (Noah).

Eventually Ibraham knew it was time to leave Hajar and the baby Isma'il. Ibrahim gave them a bag of dates and a leather flask of water. He turned to go.

The Zamzam well is now enclosed in a chamber underneath the courtyard of the sacred mosque

Hajar was dismayed but she accepted that Ibrahim was leaving them in the care of Allah. She prayed and waited. Time passed. Nothing happened. Isma'il was dying of thirst and though his mother, Hajar, was also thirsty and exhausted, she ran frantically seven times between two hills, Safa and Marwah, looking for water and trying to see if there was any help coming. Time was running out but she did not give up hope in Allah.

The angel Jibril appeared and showed Hajar a spring, now known as the Zamzam well, where the feet of the dying child, Isma'il, had scuffed the sand. The searching was over.

'Stop! Stop!' said Hajar, 'Zam! Zam!' and the well received its name. Another possible origin of the name is that it resembles the sound of rushing water.

Hajar made a rim of soil to catch the water. Birds came to drink. Hajar and her son spent five lonely days there. On the sixth day, some of the Jurhum tribe, who were nomads in the region, saw the birds. They recognised that this was a sign of water. To their surprise, they found not only water but Hajar and her son and they welcomed them into their tribe. They agreed, however, that the oasis with its spring of water would always belong to Isma'il and his descendants, the Ishma'ilites.

There are other stories remembered on Hajj which also concern Ibrahim and Isma'il.

One well-known story about Ibrahim concerns his obedience and his trust in Allah.

Ibrahim had vowed to put Allah first in his life. He was willing to sacrifice everything to God. So God decided to test him.

In a dream or in a vision Allah asked Ibrahim to sacrifice his son Isma'il. When Abraham told his son, the boy bravely accepted his fate. *'O my father! Do as thou art commanded,'* (Surah 37:102). They set out towards the place of sacrifice. Shaytan (the Devil) appeared on the way in human form and he tempted them three times not to go through with the sacrifice. Isma'il threw stones at the Devil and refused to give in. When they reached the place of sacrifice, Isma'il did not even need to be tied down. He lay face down and waited. At the last minute Allah stopped Ibrahim and Ibrahim slaughtered a ram as a sacrifice instead.

Ibrahim's faith had been tested. Allah did not want him to sacrifice his son but Ibrahim had to be willing to do so. The point is that believers must be prepared to give up everything for God. Ibrahim was rewarded with a second son. The mother was Sarah and her son Ishaq (Isaac) became the founder of the Jews. It is not clear in the Qur'anic account where the sacrifice of Isma'il was going to take place but Mina is the place where Muslims celebrate the stoning of the devil by Isma'il.

Many years later Ibrahim visited the area again. Sadly, Hajar had died by this time but Ibrahim was reunited with his son Isma'il who was now a grown man, respected in the community, and with a wife of his own from the Jurhum tribe. Ibrahim had been commanded to build a house and he asked Isma'il to help him. Together they searched for a place to dig. They found that under the mound they had chosen there were the remains of an earlier building, the very ruins of the shrine that Adam had built for Allah. Isma'il carried stones for Ibrahim to put in place and the stones were laid on top of each other, without mortar. When the cube shaped building became too tall, Ibrahim stood on a piece of rock to continue building and his feet left a deep mark on the rock.

The black stone

Isma'il went to find a special stone to place in the eastern corner. Traditionally, it is said that the angel Jibril showed Isma'il where to dig to find the al-Hajar al-Aswad, the black stone which fell from heaven. There are many legends about the stone that Isma'il found. Some say that Jibril brought it with him to Isma'il from heaven. Some say it was the white stone given to Adam but it has turned black because of people's sins. Others say the stone was actually on the grave of Adam on Mount Abu Qubais and moved of its own accord to the corner of the Ka'bah.

Together Ibrahim and Isma'il built the Ka'bah as a place to worship Allah, and the precious stone was set in the eastern corner of the building. It was the first real *Baitullah*, house of God. In the 4,000 years

The Ka'bah is the focal point at the centre of the Sacred Mosque (al-Masjid al-Haram Sharif). It is a stone building 15 metres high, 10 metres wide and 12 metres long. It is usually covered by a black cloth, which is called a kiswah (robe) decorated with Qur'anic verses sewn by Egyptian men in gold thread. The kiswah is replaced every year and the pieces of the old one are given to important visitors or sold as mementoes. There is one door in the northeast wall of the Ka'bah. The building is empty but for gold and silver lamps hanging from the ceiling, and during the Hajj the interior is washed with rose water. Muslims believe the Ka'bah lies directly below the throne of Allah and that it is the point where Allah began creating the earth. The Ka'bah is called the Baitullah, the House of God.

since then, the Ka'bah has been reconstructed a number of times but it is awe-inspiring to think that pilgrimage has been made to this place since the time of Ibrahim.

Allah told Ibrahim to call all the people to perform the Hajj and said:

> *... they will come to thee on foot and (mounted) on every kind of camel, lean on account of journeys through deep and distant mountain highways.*
>
> (Surah 22:27)

Ibrahim said:

> *'O my Lord! Make this city one of peace and security: and preserve me and my sons from worshipping idols.'*
>
> (Surah 14:35)

Bedouin settlements grew around the Ka'bah and the water supply, then a town and, eventually, the city of Makkah.

In 630 CE, when Muhammad ﷺ destroyed the idols in the Ka'bah, he was not starting a new religion; he was restoring a tradition that went back to Ibrahim and Isma'il and even back to Adam, the first human being, the first prophet.

FOR DISCUSSION

Muslims all over the world face the Ka'bah in Makkah when they pray. Why might a simple cube, instead of an ornate temple, be appropriate as the central point of the religion of Islam?

THE PILGRIMAGE TODAY

As the Hajj is a pilgrimage to places in Saudi Arabia, it is the Saudi government's responsibility to look after the pilgrims as well as overseeing the holy places. To cope with the vast number of pilgrims, the Saudi government has had to modernise and expand roads, buildings and amenities. There are motorways, hotels and car parks.

The old port of Jidda is now part of a modern city and it is the gateway for nearly all the pilgrims. They rest there in the Pilgrims' village before approaching their destination: Makkah. When they arrive, by foot, by bus, by taxi, the pilgrims keep repeating the Proclamation of Obedience, the *Talbiyah* prayer, which was first spoken by Muhammad ﷺ when he visited Makkah. Men shout the words with enthusiasm whilst women recite it quietly.

They are all speaking in Arabic, the language of Muhammad ﷺ, and this fact reinforces the sense of unity among the pilgrims who have come from all over the world.

A person in ihram should say the Talbiyah as often as possible, for example, at changes in location, moving from one place to another.

> *Labbayka Allahumma, Labbayk. Labbaka La Shareeka Laka Labbayk. Inna-alhamda Wan – ntimata Laka Walmuk. La Shareek Lak.*
>
> *Here I am, O Allah, here I am! I am here, O Allah without equal, Here I am! Yours is the praise, the grace and the Kingdom. No partner do you have.*

When the pilgrims arrive, they must first go to their hotel to leave their luggage. After they have rested and taken their *wudu'* (ritual ablution) the pilgrims will make their way to the mosque in which the Ka'bah is located. They will probably be under the leadership of their *mutawwif*, an official guide. The magnificent mosque, the Haram Sharif, has been enlarged so that pilgrims can pray on four floors but when the *Adhan* (call to prayer) is made, many worshippers have to be crammed into the courtyard, streets and carparks.

A pilgrim entering the Holy Mosque puts the right foot forward first and prays, *'In the name of Allah, may peace and blessings be upon the Messenger of Allah. Oh Allah, forgive me my sins and open to me the doors of Your mercy.'*

The *tawaf* is the rite in which pilgrims circumnambulate the Ka'bah. They do this seven times and as some people finish, others take their place.

Muslims who have been on Hajj say that it is impossible unless you have been there to imagine the numbers of people or the sense of excitement in the air. When the believers, like a vast sea, circle the Ka'bah, the atmosphere is electric. It is the only time Muslims pray in a circle instead of in rows, and it symbolises the truth that Allah is the centre of life.

Day and night, stopping only for the five prayer times, the ummah, the Muslim community, circles the Ka'bah praying to and praising Allah.

A green light has been erected on the structure of the mosque opposite the black stone and there is a line on the floor so that pilgrims know where to begin the tawaf. The pilgrims walk anti-clockwise round the Ka'bah seven times (three times quickly and four times slowly), saying their prayers. They keep the Ka'bah to their left. This is the same direction that the earth turns and the sun moves. Whole groups cling to each other as they are swept round the circuit in a human whirlpool. The elderly and the infirm are carried shoulder high on special chairs.

Pilgrims can recite a different prayer at the beginning of each tawaf, or simply say:

> *In the name of Allah: Allah the most great. Allah alone do we praise. Glory be to Allah. There is no power, there is no strength except that of Allah.*

Then the pilgrims go to perform two rak'ah behind the Maqam Ibrahim (Ibrahim's station). A beautiful gilded glass cage covers the footmarks of Ibrahim on the stone where he stood while he built the Ka'bah. It is where he and Isma'il prayed so as the pilgrims approach, they recite:

> *and take ye the Station of Abraham as a place of prayer*
> (Surah 2:125).

During the first rak'ah Surah al-Kafirun is recited (Those who reject faith):

> *Say: O ye that reject Faith! I worship not that which ye worship, nor will ye worship that which I worship. And I will not worship that which ye have been wont to worship, nor will ye worship that which I worship. To you be your Way and to me mine.* (Surah 109)

and during the second, Surah al-Iklas (The Purity of Faith):

> *Say: He is Allah, the One and Only; Allah, the Eternal, Absolute; He begetteth not, nor is He begotten; And there is none like unto Him.* (Surah 112)

Maqam Ibrahim

The tawaf round the Ka'bah begins in the south-east corner where the black stone is encased in a silver frame. It was mounted in the frame in the seventh century. All those close to it try to touch it or to kiss it, like Muhammad ﷺ did, and the others raise their hand in salute, to greet the stone. They do not worship it. The second Khalifah 'Umar ibn al-Khattab said, *'I know you are but a stone, incapable of doing good or harm. Had I not seen the Messenger of God kiss you – may God's blessing and peace be upon him – I would not kiss you.'*

ICT FOR RESEARCH

See the circling of the Ka'bah in a web page:
http://islam.org/Mosque/

The pilgrims return to the black stone and then, in obedience to a command in Surah 2:158, which they recite, they go to the two small rocky hills of Safa and Marwah which are within Makkah. They re-enact the frantic search of Hajar, running seven times between the hills. Before starting the *Sa'y* (the running or hastening) the pilgrims drink water in an underground hall from taps which are fed from the Zamzam well. The run is said to symbolise the soul searching for Allah so that its spiritual thirst can be quenched. The pilgrims express gratitude for the love shown by mothers and the provisions made by God. They pray that they too may have patience and perseverance.

The hills are now enclosed under domes and joined by covered walkways paved in marble. There are two levels. Both levels have four lanes with two going in each direction. Provision is made for wheelchairs and stretchers in an extra central lane on the ground floor. There are green markers to show where people should run rather than walk. The hills are 420 metres apart. To go from Safa to Marwah is one sa'y and the return is another sa'y. In total the seven sa'ys are 420 metres.

This part of the Hajj route has sometimes been the scene of accidents because of the enormous number of pilgrims.

The combination of these initial tawafs and sa'ys completes the *'umrah*, the lesser pilgrimage which can be taken at any time of year. Men shave their heads, or cut their hair very short if they are near to the time of the full hajj so they can shave it later. Women clip their hair by a small amount about the length of a finger tip. 'Umrah is completed and the pilgrims may remove ihram clothing and dress normally.

Pilgrims run along the enclosed path between Safa and Marwah

Pilgrim tents on the plain of Arafat

Pilgrims waiting to complete the full pilgrimage spend their time in Makkah usually fasting, praying, reading the Qur'an, meeting other members of the ummah and attending the *Haram Shariff*.

The 8th day of Dhul-Hijjah is officially day one of the Hajj. All the pilgrims leave Makkah and travel seven kilometres east where they will camp at Mina and spend the night of the 8th of Dhul-Hijjah in prayer. Mina is not much larger than a village but encampments of tents, with toilets and washing facilities, have been erected to accommodate the millions of visitors. The tents are arranged in groups according to the area in the world from which the pilgrims have come. Safety regulations forbid cooking because there have been problems with fires, but people can buy food from street vendors or they may have brought their own provisions. The al-Khalif Mosque at Mina is the centre for prayers but because of the vast numbers of people, the majority pray outside or in their tents.

Early the next morning, on the 9th of Dhul-Hijjah, after *Fajr* (dawn) prayers, the journey continues, by foot, by bus or by some other vehicle, another twelve kilometres eastwards to the plain of Arafat. As in Mina, thousands of tents are provided to give shade in the intense heat and the Saudi government has planted trees on the wide, rocky, barren terrain.

This is the most important day of the Hajj. The pilgrims gather on the plain before Mount Arafat, which is called the Mount of Mercy. This small mountain is where Allah forgave Adam and Hawwa' and where Muhammad ﷺ preached his last *khutbah* (sermon) when he asked Allah to forgive the sins of believers. Here, from noon to sunset, the pilgrims make the *wuquf* (the stand before God) praying, meditating and concentrating on Allah alone. Each individual stands directly before Allah. If the stand is missed the Hajj is not valid. Muhammad ﷺ is reported to have said, *'The best of prayers is the prayer of the day of Arafat'* and *'The Hajj is Arafat'*.

This gathering at Arafat on the 9th of Dhul-Hijjah makes Muslims think of the Day of Judgement, but they are joyful because they believe that their repentance has been accepted, they have been cleansed by God's forgiveness and they are as sinless as the day they were born.

A Muslim woman describes the scene:

Facing Makkah, they pray to Allah in their own ways: some in groups, some alone, some outside in the searing heat, others in their tents or coaches. With hands held close to their bodies or out in front of them or stretched up to the skies, they lose themselves in prayer, repeating verses from the Holy Qur'an or speaking to Allah with simple words which well up from their hearts. Many will sob and weep.'

Istafiah is' Harc, 1999

At sunset, the pilgrims hurry eight kilometres to Muzdalifah, a flat area not quite as large as the Plain of Arafat, where they will pray the Maghrib and 'Isha' prayers, then collect forty-nine pebbles which will be needed the next day. The pebbles must be about the size of a small bean or a chick pea. Seven is the number of perfection for Muslims and this may be why seven times seven stones are needed.

That night, people rest in the open air, some sleeping, some praying.

After midnight or after Fajr prayers on the morning of the 10th day of Dhul-Hijja, the pilgrims return to Mina on the way back to Makkah. At Mina they throw pebbles at the three stone pillars which represent the three times that Shaytan, the Devil, tried to tempt Isma'il. The pilgrims shout *'In the name of God! Allah is Almighty!'* as they stone the three *Jamrah* (pillars). This symbolises their total rejection of the Devil. It also strengthens their dedication and their resolve to resist evil and to follow Allah more devoutly.

After the stoning of the first pillar, the pilgrims who can afford it will sacrifice a sheep, a goat or a camel to remember that Ibrahim had been willing to make an extreme sacrifice and to show that they, too, are willing to obey Allah. The pilgrims have already

Stoning the Devil is done with energetic enthusiasm, shouting the Takbir: 'Allahu Akbar!' 'Allah is the Greatest'. On the first day at Mina, seven stones are thrown at the largest pillar only. All three pillars are stoned in the afternoon of the following days. It is not permissible to start before noon. The one furthest from Makkah is to be stoned, then the middle one and finally Jamrah al-Aqabah.

shown their willingness to make sacrifices by coming on the pilgrimage. Back at home their families and communities will be thinking of the pilgrims, remembering the same stories of Ibrahim and will also be celebrating the Hajj by sacrificing an animal. This sacrifice is part of Id-ul-Adha (the feast of sacrifice) celebrated by all Muslims all over the world. Many animals are sacrificed at Hajj. Part of the meat is eaten and part given to the poor, though pilgrims may choose to give away all of the meat. Nowadays the Saudi government has to make special arrangements to deal with the large number of carcases and the excess meat. There are large facilities for freezing and preserving meat and distribution networks throughout the Muslim world.

After the sacrifice the men may have their heads shaved as a symbol of new beginnings and the women trim their hair by at least two and a half centimetres. This denotes that ihram is over and they are free from all the restrictions. Three days may be spent at Mina and the Hajj ends officially on the 13th of Dhul-Hijjah. During the last days many return to Makkah for another seven circuits of the Ka'bah.

At the end of Hajj, some buy water from the Zamzam well. They dip their white cloths in it and these cloths, which are kept as treasured possessions, will be used later as shrouds when eventually the pilgrims die and are buried. They drink as much of the water as possible because it is believed to have healing properties, and they take bottles of it home.

Some extend their stay and go on to al-Madinah to visit the tomb of Muhammad ﷺ, or to other places which are important in Islam; but this extension is not part of the official Hajj.

On completion of the Hajj, the male pilgrims are *Hajji* and the females take the title *Hajja*. The pilgrims have fulfilled their promise and have completed their once-in-a-lifetime journey.

Some pilgrims, in fact, repeat the journey many times and even make the journey when they are very old. To die on Hajj is regarded as a blessing from Allah.

IN YOUR NOTES

Write a few sentences to explain:
- why being on the Mount of Mercy on the 9th of Dhul-Hijjah might be the most important appointment in a Muslim's life.
- the ways in which the Hajj could be a symbol of life's journey
- why it is appropriate for the ihram sheets to be used as a burial shroud.

THE ROLE OF PILGRIMAGE IN SPIRITUAL DEVELOPMENT

The word 'pilgrimage' means to set out with a definite purpose.

It is a physical journey and it is a spiritual journey. The experience of pilgrimage helps believers in any faith to learn more about their religion and to understand more about their beliefs.

Pilgrimage is one of the Five Pillars of Islam. It is a duty for Muslims so the purpose for going on the Hajj is also to perform an act of *'ibadah* (an act of worship, submission and obedience). The discipline of being obedient, for Muslims, is important itself but there are many other benefits for the pilgrim in going on Hajj.

Nowadays people take travel for granted and, though it can still be dangerous, expensive and full of inconveniences, it is difficult to imagine what travelling might have been like at the time of Muhammad ﷺ.

The most obvious benefit for Muslims in going on Hajj is that they will have a glimpse of what life must have been like in the times of the Prophet. Muhammad ﷺ was a trader for much of his life. He was used to long journeys. The caravans of camels carrying oriental goods would travel when it was cool. The travellers would look for shade in the heat of the day and they would know the importance of keeping to an established route, a sure way that avoids the pitfalls and perils of the journey.

Not only will pilgrims on Hajj learn about the conditions of such travelling, but they may gain insight into the language of the Qur'an. The first Surah promises *'the straight way'* which believers must follow throughout their lives. The symbol of Islam, the star and crescent moon which guide travellers on their way, may grow in significance for the pilgrims.

The physical hardship of the journey develops courage and perseverance, whilst even the preparations teach various aspects of self-control. The journey develops faith and trust in Allah.

This spiritual dimension of the journey is expressed in the prayers used on the Hajj, as in the words of this prayer which is one of those used on entering Makkah:

> *O Allah, this sanctuary is Your sacred place and this city is Your city and this slave is Your slave. I have come to You from a distant land, carrying all my sins and misdeeds as an afflicted person seeking Your help and dreading Your punishment. I beg You to accept me and grant me Your complete forgiveness and give me permission to enter Your vast garden of delight.*

The following is the prayer traditionally recited for the seventh tawaf and it petitions for faith and other spiritual gifts that will last not just for the pilgrimage but for life:

> *O Allah! I ask of Thee perfect faith, true conviction and a heart full of devotion towards Thee, a tongue busy in remembering Thee, vast provision, and lawful and clean earnings, sincere repentance and repentance before death, peace at the time of death and Thy forgiveness.*

Any person who goes on a journey is likely to be affected by the experience. The effects may be negative; they may be positive; they may be small; they may influence different aspects of life; or the journey may be a catalyst that provokes an enormous life-enhancing change.

Pilgrimage is meant to play a part in the spiritual development of a Muslim and there may be a change in the hajji (or hajja) on the return home. Their

personal religious commitment may be deeper and their behaviour towards other people may be more considerate because they will have had to cultivate tolerance for individuals with whom they have travelled. The experience of seeing the Ummah in its diversity of race and culture, and yet the equality of its members and the unity of purpose, may have had a profound effect on the pilgrim.

There were then thousands of pilgrims, from all over the world. They were of all colours, from blue-eyed blonds to black-skinned Africans but we were all participating in the same ritual, displaying a spirit of unity and brotherhood that my experiences in America had led me to believe never could exist between the whites and the non-whites. And in the words and in the actions and in the deeds of the 'white' Muslims, I felt the same sincerity that I felt among the black African Muslims of Nigeria, Sudan and Ghana.

From the Autobiography of Malcolm X

Malcolm X

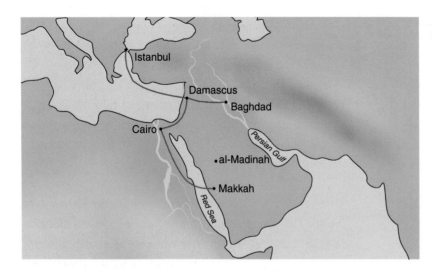

The ancient caravan routes

The Five Pillars all encourage discipline but their purpose is more than that. They each have a role in a Muslim's spiritual development. Each one reinforces a Muslim's awareness, in a changing world, of Allah who never changes. They each also reaffirm the equality of believers and the continuity of the faith over the ages.

Until the nineteenth century, travelling the long distance to Makkah usually meant being part of a caravan. There were three main caravans which pilgrims joined on the route:

- Egyptian – which formed in Cairo;
- Iraqi – which set out from Baghdad;
- Syrian – which, after 1453, started not simply from Damascus but came from Istanbul.

The journey took months. For some pilgrims it took years. Some ran out of money and left the caravan to work for a while. Bandits, disease and the rough terrain meant that some never completed their physical journey and never returned home.

FOR DISCUSSION

Consider the extent to which going on the Hajj:
- Reinforces the awareness of Allah
- Strengthens Ummah.

STUDY THIS PASSAGE

Study this passage from the Qur'an. Think about its meaning and choose a short quotation you might learn and use in an essay about the Hajj:

Behold! We gave the site, to Abraham, of the (Sacred) House, (saying): 'Associate not anything (in worship) with Me; and sanctify My House for those who compass it round, or stand up, or bow, or prostrate themselves (therein in prayer).

'And proclaim the Pilgrimage among men: they will come to thee on foot and (mounted) on every kind of camel, lean on account of journeys through deep and distant mountain highways;

'That they may witness the benefits (provided) for them, and celebrate the name of Allah, through the Days appointed, over the cattle which He has provided for them (for sacrifice): then eat ye thereof and feed the distressed ones in want.'   (Surah 22:26–28)

PRACTICE EXAMINATION QUESTIONS

1 (a) Describe the Five Pillars. (8 marks)

The essential facts about each of the Five Pillars should be covered. See the general account in Chapter one.

(b) Explain the importance of the Hajj for Muslims. (7 marks)

Some facts about the journey may be helpful but the importance of the Hajj is the area to concentrate on. Make your points address the actual question.

(c) 'The Hajj unites Muslims more than any other of the Five Pillars.'

Do you agree? Give reasons to support your answer and show that you have thought about other points of view. (5 marks)

Refer to points you have made earlier in the question as evidence to support your arguments. You are not meant to be discussing the importance of the Hajj but whether or not it unites the ummah and, if so, more than any other one pillar. Support your decision with evidence. Consider other points of view. If you decide all the pillars are equal for Muslims you must give reasons and think of reasons why people might disagree with you.

2 (a) Describe what happens from when the pilgrims first arrive at Mina during the Hajj to the return to Makkah. (8 marks)

You have been asked to limit your description to the last part of the Hajj so obviously you need to include as much detail as possible.

(b) Explain the significance of the events you have described. (7 marks)

Try to place the material appropriately to illustrate the explanation you are giving about the significance.

(c) 'Pilgrimage is a waste of time and money.'

Do you agree? Give reasons to support your answer and show that you have thought about other points of view. You must refer to Islam in your answer. (5 marks)

You are free to come to any conclusion but you are expected to support your view with sensible reasons. You should refer to both time and money. It is permissible to agree with part of the quotation or to question the implications of the wording. You are meant to be responding with reference to Islam so your debate may home in on the Hajj immediately or you may wish to refer to pilgrimage in general to make points about intentions of religious practices. Consider the extent to which all Muslims themselves would hold the same views as each other.

3 (a) Describe how Muslims prepare for Hajj. (8 marks)

Description of ihram is required, not just the arrangements for the journey, but remember to include the spiritual preparations too.

(b) Explain why Muslims go on Hajj. (7 marks)

Stop and think before you begin. Make a list of reasons, then keep looking at the question so you can address it properly.

(c) 'In modern times, the pilgrimage to Makkah is the least important of the five duties Muhammad ﷺ set for Muslims.'

Do you agree? Give reasons to support your answer and show that you have thought about other points of view. (5 marks)

Modern times must be referred to and the attitudes of Muslims should be discussed with accurate knowledge and sensitive understanding so that the discussion makes sense. The question is structured so you may find yourself referring back to points you raised earlier in the answer. After all, if people make such an effort to prepare and if the reasons for going on the pilgrimage were explained fully in part (b), then it is no wonder there is relevance in this practice even in the twenty-first century.

5

PLACES AND FORMS OF WORSHIP

The ways in which Muslim artefacts are used in the practicalities of worship. A consideration of the ways in which these artefacts might support and influence the beliefs and attitudes of the worshippers:

- **the design and artefacts of a mosque, especially the minaret, dome, *mihrab* (niche), *qiblah* (direction), *minbar* (steps for sermon) and calligraphy;**

- **the absence of any representations of Allah or Muhammad ﷺ;**

- **the different ways in which the mosque is used by the community;**

- **the role of the *imam*;**

- **Salah and du'a;**

- **the use of artefacts in private worship, e.g. beads, prayer mats.**

FOR DISCUSSION

What artefacts would a traveller need in order to fulfil these three conditions?

Allah can be worshipped anywhere

In some religions there is a wide variety of places and forms of worship.

In Islam, the outward appearance of the places of worship may vary from a converted house to an enormous elegant building with fountains and marble courtyards, but there are features in common in the design of all the buildings, and the form of worship is similar worldwide.

> *To Allah belong the East and the West; whithersoever ye turn, there is Allah's countenance.*
>
> (Surah 2.116).
>
> *The whole earth has been made a place of prostration for me.*
> ('prostration' means to bow down in worship)

Muhammad said, *'Wherever the time of prayer overtakes you, pray: that place is a mosque.'*

Muslims, therefore, do not need a building in order to worship Allah. They can pray in any clean place.

Three important conditions were laid down by Muhammad ﷺ concerning prayer:

- Pray in a clean place
- Pray at five set times a day
- Pray facing Makkah, the holy city.

The Qur'an recommends praying with other believers:

> *And be steadfast in prayer; practise regular charity; and bow down your heads with those who bow down (in worship).*
>
> (Surah 2:43)

It also recommends praying regularly:

> *'Verily, I am Allah; there is no god but I: so serve thou Me (only), and establish regular prayer for celebrating My praise.'*
>
> (Surah 20:14)

The building of a place for these communal prayers is one of the first things a Muslim community does. The Muslim place of worship is called a mosque or a masjid (place of prostration).

Muhammad ﷺ set the example by building the first mosque when he set up the first Muslim community in 622 CE in al-Madinah. Muhammad ﷺ let his camel stop where it wanted and there he built his house and the first place of worship. It was not the first place ever built for the worship of Allah. That was the Ka'bah, built thousands of years before, in Makkah. Muhammad ﷺ taught his followers to face the Ka'bah when they prayed. The rituals which Muhammad ﷺ established in al-Madinah have been the pattern for Muslim prayers ever since and the whole procedure of worship is rich with symbolism.

In Britain, many mosques are in converted houses

THE DESIGN OF A MOSQUE

The call to prayer

FOR DISCUSSION

- Why do you think the star and crescent is used as the symbol of Islam?
- How appropriate is it as a symbol of Islam?

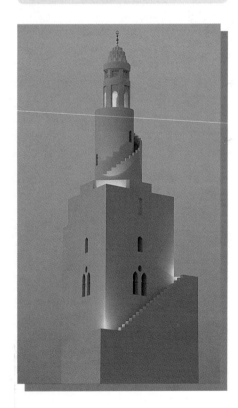

A minaret in al-Madinah

Everything about a mosque supports and influences the beliefs and attitudes of the worshippers. Prostration is not only worshipping Allah by praying. Prostration is a whole life spent in submission to Allah and complete obedience to the Qur'an. Every feature in the mosque reinforces this commitment. The whole mosque could be described as a symbol of the Muslim faith and the features of both the exterior and the interior have symbolic meanings.

Some mosques are easy to identify from the outside because they have domes and towers called minarets.

They may also have a crescent shaped moon on top and sometimes a five pointed star. The star and crescent is a symbol of the Islamic religion, which is used on the stamps and flags of Muslim countries.

THE MINARET

In Muslim countries, the Mu'adhdhin (muezzin) calls the believers to prayer five times daily from the minaret. He stands facing the Ka'bah in Makkah. Sometimes, however, the call to prayer is recorded and played through loud speakers.

The call to prayer is in Arabic and begins, *'Allahu Akbar'*, *'Allah is the Greatest'*. The *Adhan* is the call to prayer and in *Fajr* (the morning prayer) includes the words, *'Prayer is better than sleep'*. Non-Muslim visitors to Muslim countries often find the call to prayer very haunting, atmospheric and moving. The words echo over city roofs or linger on the desert air. How much more it must mean to a Muslim visitor who normally lives in a country where the call to prayer is not allowed.

The dome of a mosque symbolises the universe

Inside the prayer hall, just before worship begins, the Mu'adhdhin repeats the call with slightly different words. This call is the '*Iqamah* and it includes the statement that prayer is about to begin. The Mu'adhdhin stands with the worshippers on the front row. Everyone is shoulder to shoulder facing Makkah.

THE DOME

The dome symbolises the universe which Allah created and over which he rules. Some mosques have four minarets and a dome. Together these are said to represent the Five Pillars of Islam. The dome allows the air to circulate and it amplifies the human voice. The circulation of air, particularly in hot countries, helps the worshippers to concentrate on their prayers and the amplification helps them to hear the sermon.

Sometimes the domes are beautifully decorated both outside and inside. In keeping with the beliefs of Islam, mosques should not be made of expensive materials, but this does not mean they should be plain and ordinary.

Before entering the area where Muslims pray, there is always a place for ritual washing. This is a necessary part of the design of a mosque because it is important to approach Allah in a state of purity. The ceremonial washing is called *wudu'* (see preparations for prayer on page 74).

The facilities for wudu' may be provided in a splendid courtyard with fountains of running water or they may consist of a simple sink with taps. There will probably be separate amenities for men and for women. There will also be somewhere for shoes to be left outside the praying area.

Wudu is an essential preparation for prayer

The interior of a mosque is sometimes difficult to describe. It may look very simple, and even bare, though the walls may be inlaid with precious materials and the carpet beautifully patterned to look like indivdual prayer mats. In hot countries, the mosque may not even be indoors.

There are some features, however, which are common to all prayer halls.

The area for prayer is the heart of the mosque and plenty of space is needed because it is a place for prostration. There are no chairs in a prayer hall. No furniture is needed apart from the *minbar* (set of steps) from which the imam preaches the Friday *khutbah* (sermon). There is something about the design of the building, however, which is very important. One wall is very special. It is called the *qiblah* (direction) wall and in it is the *mihrab*.

The mihrab and minbar

THE MIHRAB AND THE QIBLAH

The mihrab is a niche, a sort of alcove, which shows that this is the quiblah wall, the wall indicating the direction of the Ka'bah in Makkah. The Ka'bah is said to be the oldest place of worship in the world (see page 53 for how it was built by Adam and restored by Ibrahim (peace be unto them).). Even when praying at home, Muslims have a picture or a text from the Qur'an on a wall showing the qiblah so they know which way to face in their prayers. Muslims often carry a compass with them, particularly when they are on a journey. It is not simply for them to find their way; it is for finding the direction of Makkah at the times of prayer.

THINKING POINT

Where is the direction of Makkah from where you are as you read this book?

At the beginning of his preaching, Muhammad ﷺ encouraged his followers to face Jerusalem as the Jews did, but in 624 CE at al-Madinah, as a result of a revelation about the true qiblah, he changed the direction of prayer to Makkah.

THE MINBAR

The minbar is the stand or platform, in the praying area, from which the imam delivers his khutbah, speech or sermon, at Salat-ul-Jumu'ah, Friday prayers. There are usually at least three steps and he stands half way up as a sign of humility before Allah and equality with his fellow Muslims. Sometimes there is a special seat for the imam.

CALLIGRAPHY

Another significant feature of a mosque is that there are no pictures, statues or images. This is because, from the very beginning, Islam has been against idolatry. When Muhammad ﷺ rode into Makkah in 629 CE and destroyed the idols of wood and stone in the Ka'bah, it was an important moment. The cleansing of the Ka'bah represented a key belief in Islam; a belief that had been held by the ancient prophets before Muhammad ﷺ but which had been forgotten; the belief that Allah has no partner.

Only Allah is to be worshipped. To make an image would be *shirk* (association), the terrible sin of regarding something as equal to Allah. People would soon forget that pictures and statues are only representations and start to worship them as idols.

Another reason why there are no likenesses of Allah is because Allah is beyond human imagining and too great to be portrayed by human hands.

To make an image of any living person or animal would also be insulting Allah because Allah is the sole creator. Some Muslims are more strict than others and they forbid all representations of the human form including photography.

In the mosque, instead of statues and pictures, decorative patterns are used. Sometimes they are made of mosaic tiles and precious stones. The patterns are abstract, geometric or taken from plant life but they are deliberately not realistic. The more two-dimensional the better. In this way there is no risk of an image becoming an object of worship in place of Allah.

The concentration on patterns has led to a deeper understanding of the principles of geometry and other

Islamic calligraphy from the Qur'an, in the shape of a 'ship of life', which reads: 'I believe in Allah, and His angels, His books, His prophets, the Last Day, predestination, good and evil, and resurrection after death'.

branches of mathematics, and Islamic architecture has been an inspiration for many other cultures.

Often the patterns are decorative designs made up of calligraphy with declarations in Arabic which are the very words of Allah from the Qur'an.

This beautiful writing is done in different styles. Sometimes it is so elaborate and intricate that the Arabic is difficult to read.

ICT FOR RESEARCH

Design a similar pattern using a computer.

FOR DISCUSSION

Do you think it is right to spend a lot of money on a place of worship?

The arabesque geometric designs are sometimes of interweaving leaves in a floral pattern. They reflect the balance and harmony in Allah's universe.

THE MOSQUE IN THE COMMUNITY

The first mosque in al-Madinah was like other buildings of the time. Muhammad ﷺ had huts for himself and his wives around a central courtyard where the Muslims met for prayer, business was conducted and visitors camped.

In the United Kingdom the mosques serve many functions for the community as well as being places of prayer. It is the *madrassah* (school) where children learn Arabic and how to recite the Qur'an. They also learn English and other languages such as Urdu. There may be a reading room, a library and a bookshop. The prayer hall itself may be used for teaching. It is also used for funeral services, but not for weddings. There may be a mortuary for laying out the dead and preparing the corpse for burial. The mosque may also serve as a lawcourt for the community. There will be kitchens and community rooms, maybe even games rooms. More recently-constructed mosques are purpose-built to accommodate the full range of community activities.

THE ROLE OF THE IMAM

All Muslims are equal in the sight of Allah. '*Imam*' means 'in the front' and the imam, who can be a woman if there are no men present, is simply the person who stands at the front, facing the qiblah, to lead the prayers. Behind him or her, the whole *jumu'ah* (congregation or assembly) in rows, shoulder to shoulder, also faces the qiblah.

It is important not to confuse the word 'imam' with the word '*iman*' which is the Arabic word for faith or belief.

The imam is not usually paid, certainly not for leading the prayers, though he may earn money as caretaker or secretary of the mosque. He may earn his living from a job outside the mosque.

Large mosques may have a full-time paid imam and sometimes more than one imam because the building and the activities require much supervision. There are no priests, monks or nuns in Islam, so the imam is not ordained as a holy man. His role may still be a vocation, however, because he will feel that Allah has called him to do this work. The word 'teacher' is often used for the role of the imam and this does describe some aspects of his work. He teaches Arabic, he is well-versed in the meaning of the Qur'an and the hadith, he gives religious advice and he may preside over or organise religious festivals. He is the *khatib* who preaches the khutbah at Salat-ul-Jumu'ah, the themes of which may be of importance for ordinary Muslim life and local politics, and he may preside over discussions and matters of Muslim Shari'ah law. He can officiate at name-giving and marriage, though other members of the jumu'ah may also conduct these ceremonies.

The title 'Imam' is used by Shi'ah Muslims in a special way. See page 37.

THE USE OF ARTEFACTS IN PRIVATE WORSHIP

In many religions, people use artefacts to help them concentrate during their private devotions. Muslims do not have statues and they do not feel the need for shrines, pictures, candles and incense in the home. They do, however, have some artefacts which aid their worship.

BEADS

> The most beautiful names belong to Allah: so call on him by them.

Some Muslims find that a set of prayer beads is useful for keeping count when they are reciting the 99 beautiful names of Allah. *Subhah* is an Arabic word for the actual beads and *tasbih* is a Turkish word for using the beads. The string may have 33 beads or the full 99 separated into three groups by extra, larger beads. (See page 4)

Not all Muslims use prayer beads. They are, however, particularly important in Sufism, which is a mystical approach to Islam, and many other Muslims have borrowed Sufi techniques for reciting phrases in praise of Allah.

A Muslim compass showing the direction of Makkah

CLOCKS AND COMPASSES

Muslims can pray to Allah anywhere when they obey the command to pray five times daily. Sometimes this is in the mosque but often it is at home. The essential factors are that at the set times they should face Makkah and pray in a clean place.

They need, therefore, a means of telling the time, especially if they are in a non-Muslim country where the call to prayer is not allowed by the local by-laws, and they need to know the direction of Makkah.

The times are not exactly at sunrise, noon and sunset because it is important that Muslims should not seem to be worshipping the sun. They worship the creator of the sun, Allah, and they use sunrise and sunset to calculate the times of prayer. The prayers are to be said between certain times:

- *Fajr* (between dawn and sunrise)
- *Zuhr* (after mid-day)
- *'Asr* (between late afternoon and sunset)
- *Maghrib* (between sunset and the end of daylight)
- *'Isha'* (night, until dawn).

ICT FOR RESEARCH

Visit: www.ummah.net to see Islamic calendars with prayer times for cities near where you live.

At home, the qiblah is marked, perhaps by a poster of the Ka'bah in Makkah, so the Muslim household know which way to face. Rather than seeing the five times daily commitment as a difficult rule or a tedious routine, many Muslims welcome the regular refreshing short break from the routines of daily life.

The clean place is catered for by having a prayer mat.

PRAYER MATS

Because the Prophet spoke against the artistic representation of humans and animals, geometric patterns often dominate the designs of Muslims. Although Persia embraced the Islamic Shi'ite religion, the area's carpet-makers often continued to decorate their creations with lively animal and human figures in dream-like surroundings. On the other hand, it is quite rare to find any animal or human figures on early Turkish rugs.

Turkish prayer rugs are characterized by rich and minutely detailed decoration. Found on all prayer rugs is the arched mihrab, or prayer niche, which is pointed to Makkah when the rugs are used in prayer.

If Muslims are not able to say their prayers at the correct time for a valid reason, they can say a number of prayers together at the next set time, but they are not allowed to say them early. In the United Kingdom, working people may take half an hour in the evening catching up with their prayers.

ICT FOR RESEARCH

Visit www.ummah to find our more about prayer mats and their designs.

FOR DISCUSSION

- If God knows everything, why do people pray?
- Can prayer change things?
- Do you think Muslims in non-Muslim countries should be allowed to make the call to prayer from the mosque?

Prayer at home

SALAH

Salah (prayer) is *fard* (obligatory). It is one of the Five Pillars of Islam.

> *Muhammad ﷺ said, 'If one of you had a river right by his door and he bathed in it five times a day, do you think that there would be any dirt left on him?' They said, 'Not a trace'. He said, 'That is how it is with the five prayers; by means of them God washes away all sins.*
>
> (Hadith)

On the night journey to al-Quds (Jerusalem) when Muhammad ﷺ visited heaven, the number of times when Muslims must pray was set by Allah as five times a day.

The Qur'an recommends prayer:

> *So (give) glory to Allah, when ye reach eventide and when ye rise in the morning; Yea, to Him be praise, in the heavens and on earth; and in the late afternoon and when the day begins to decline.*
>
> (Surah 30:17–18)
>
> *So woe to the worshippers who are neglectful of their Prayers.*
>
> (Surah 107:4–5)
>
> *…celebrate (constantly) the praises of thy Lord before the rising of the sun, and before its setting; yea, celebrate them for part of the hours of the night, and at the sides of the day: that thou mayest have (spiritual) joy.*
>
> (Surah 20:130).

It also recommends that prayer should be done with sincere intentions and should be accompanied by good deeds:

> *Those who (want but) to be seen (of men), but refuse (to supply) (even) neighbourly needs.*
>
> (Surah 107:6–7).

PREPARATIONS FOR SALAH

> *O Children of Adam! Wear your beautiful apparel at every time and place of prayer.*
>
> (Surah 7:31).

Prayer is such a special occasion that not only should the place be clean but the worshipper should prepare with a ritual sequence of ablutions called *wudu'*, which means 'to wash'.

- First the person says, *'In the name of Allah, the Compassionate, the Merciful'.*
- The hands are washed.
- The mouth is rinsed three times.
- Water is sniffed into the nostrils then blown out. This is done three times.
- The face is washed three times using both hands.
- The right arm and then the left is washed three times.
- The hair neck and ears are wiped over with wet hands.
- The right foot and then the left is washed to the ankle.
- Finally, the person makes the declaration of faith: *'I bear witness that there is no god but Allah, and Muhammad ﷺ is the Messenger of Allah.'*

The outward cleanliness symbolises inner purity of the heart and soul which is necessary if a Muslim is entering the presence of Allah who is holy and pure. If travellers are in the desert and cannot find water they are permitted to use sand. They touch the sand with both hands then wipe the hands over the face and up the arms to the elbows. This version of the cleansing is called *tayammum* in Arabic. It shows that the meaning of ritual ablutions is important and the washing, though of value for the sake of cleanliness, is mostly significant as a symbol of the purifying of the soul.

It is not necessary to perform wudu' for every prayer time unless the worshipper has fallen asleep meantime or has been to the lavatory since the previous prayer time. It is not necessary to keep washing the feet except for the first prayer each day if

Prayers in the mosque

socks or stockings are worn. Sometimes *ghusl*, a full bath, is required before prayer if the Muslim has had sexual intercourse.

After washing, Muslims cover their heads before praying. Men wear a small cap called a *topi* and women wear a *burka* which is a shawl draped over their heads and shoulders. They are ready now to express their *niyyah*, their silent intention to offer salah.

Worshippers must face Makkah which is indicated by the mihrab in the qiblah wall. They stand in rows behind the leader of the prayers who is also facing the direction of the Ka'bah.

> *We see the turning of thy face (for guidance) to the heavens: now shall We turn thee to a qiblah that shall please thee. Turn then thy face in the direction of the Sacred Mosque: wherever ye are, turn your faces in that direction.*   (Surah 2:144)

The Old Dehli Jamia Mosque in India

The leader gives the timing of the actions so they are made in unison.

Public participation tends to be mostly for men in the older Islamic countries, especially on Fridays at noon when prayer at the mosque is compulsory.

In some mosques there is a separate section for women; in others, there is an area behind the men. This is to protect the modesty of the women as they perform the movements and to stop the men being distracted. However, in some African countries there is hardly any segregation, not even for ablutions.

PERFORMING SALAT

Salat consists of an introduction, two or four cycles of movements according to the time of day.

- Fajr 2
- Zuhr 4
- 'Asr 4
- Maghrib 3
- 'Isha' 4

Each cycle is called a *rak'ah* and is made up of a routine involving reciting whilst standing (*qiyam*), bowing (*ruku*) or prostrating (*sajda*).

THE INTRODUCTION:

- To begin, the worshipper stands upright, raises hands to the level of his ears and says the takbir, the acknowledgement of greatness:

> *Allahu Akbar*
> (Allah is the greatest)

All distractions from outside and from inside the person are put aside.

- Then the opening surah of the Qur'an is recited. This is al-Fatihah.

> *In the name of Allah, Most Gracious, Most Merciful,*
> *Praise be to Allah, the Cherisher and Sustainer of the Worlds,*
> *Most Gracious, Most Merciful;*
> *Master of the Day of Judgement,*
> *Thee do we worship,*
> *And Thine aid we seek.*
> *Show us the straight way.*
> *The way of those on whom*
> *Thou hast bestowed Thy Grace,*
> *Those whose (portion)*
> *Is not wrath,*
> *And who go not astray.*

Al-Fatihah is called the mother of the Qur'an.

- The introduction is completed by the recitation of one or more surahs.

THE FIRST RAK'AH

- The first cycle begins with another acknowledgement of the greatness of Allah. Then the right hand is placed over the left just below the chest and the worshipper says:

> *O Allah, glory and praise are for You and blessed is Your name and exalted is Your Majesty. There is no God but You. I seek shelter from the rejected Shaytan.*

- Bowing as a sign of respect, the worshipper bends forwards with hands on knees and says, *'Allahu Akbar'*, *'Allah is the greatest'* and then three times, *'Glory to my Lord the Almighty'*.
- Standing upright again, the person says:

> *Allah hears those who praise Him.*
> *Our Lord, praise be to You.*

The Prayer positions

- Saying aloud, *'Allahu Akbar'*, the worshipper prostrates him or herself on the ground with forehead, nose, palms of both hands, knees and big toes touching the floor. The following words are recited three times, *'Glory to My Lord, the Most High'*. The worshipper sits back on the heels with the palms of the hands placed on the knees. This is a moment of rest and then the worshipper repeats the prostration of total submission to Allah.
- The worshipper returns to the standing position with the words, *'Allahu Akbar'*. One rak'ah has been completed.

THE SECOND RAK'AH

- The second cycle is the same as the first except that afterwards the worshipper sits back with the left foot bent towards the right one and hands resting on the knees whilst reciting the Declaration and then a two rak'ah prayer honouring the Prophet Muhammad ﷺ and his family.
The *At Tashahhud*, the Declaration, is as follows:

All prayer is for Allah, all worship and goodness.

Peace be upon you O Prophet, and the mercy of Allah And His blessings.

Peace be upon us and on the righteous servants of Allah.

I bear witness that there is no god but Allah.

I bear witness that Muhammad ﷺ is His servant and messenger.

When the correct number of rak'ahs for the time of day have been completed, the worshipper turns the head to the right and then to the left, blessing fellow Muslims with the words, *'Peace be on you and Allah's blessings'*. The Muslim may also be greeting the two angels which sit, one on each shoulder, recording the good and bad deeds which believers commit.

According to the Hadith, Muhammad ﷺ said prayer performed in company is twenty-seven times

FOR DISCUSSION

- For what other reasons might prayer strengthen Muslims as individuals and as a community?
- What are the advantages and disadvantages of set times and set routines for prayer?
- Approximately how many times a year does a Muslim pray?

better than prayer performed alone. Wherever a Muslim travels in the world, the prayers of the ummah are the same. Any Muslim can join in anywhere and feel at home among strangers. This is one reason why prayer helps to strengthen Muslim unity.

DU'A

Salah is formal prayer. It is in Arabic. When salah is completed, the Muslim raises his or her hands with palms upwards and Du'a commences. Du'a is personal prayer. The word in Arabic means 'asking'.

I listen to the prayer of every suppliant when he calleth on Me.

(Surah 2:186)

The worshipper may stay seated after salah and pray in his or her own language. They may recite extra rak'ahs or parts of the Qur'an. They may use prayer beads. At the end of Du'a the believer wipes the hands across the face to show that the blessing of Allah has been received.

Du'a may be prayed anytime; it is the cry from the heart.

If ye fear (an enemy), pray on foot, or riding (as may be most convenient).

(Surah 2:239)

PRACTICE EXAMINATION QUESTIONS

1 (a) **Describe fully how a Muslim prepares for prayer. (8 marks)**

A full description would include details of Wudu' but do not forget to mention the obvious preparations such as covering the head and facing Makkah.

(b) **Explain the meaning of the movements during prayer. (7 marks)**

In order to explain the meaning some description of the movements is necessary but concentrate on the meaning of each action and of salat as a whole.

(c) **'Prayer is never a waste of time.'**

Do you agree? Give reasons to support your opinion and show you have thought about different points of view. You must refer to Islam in your answer. (5 marks)

Before you begin this part, look back at what you have written about the preparations for prayer and the meaning of the rak'ahs. This might give you some ideas for reasons to support the statement and reasons to disagree with it before you come to a final conclusion. Do not forget to consider whether or not the points you make apply not only to prayer in general but also to Muslim prayer.

2 (a) **Describe the significant features in the prayer area of a mosque. (8 marks)**

Remember that the description may include what is not there such as statues.

(b) **Explain how salah (prayer) might affect the life of a Muslim. (7 marks)**

It is easy to think of the disadvantages of set times of prayer especially for a Muslim in a non-Muslim country, but the question requires some understanding of the positive benefits that regular prayer might have on the religious growth of a Muslim and the effects which the constant reminders of the solidarity of the ummah might have on a Muslim's relationship with others.

(c) **'Prayer is the most important of the Five Pillars of Islam.'**

Do you agree? Give reasons to support your opinion and show you have thought about different points of view. (5 marks)

You may wish to argue that prayer is the most important but you also need to consider points that might be made in favour of the other pillars. You may wish to argue that the Five Pillars are all equal to a Muslim but do not forget to refer to the wording of the statement in the question.

3 (a) **Describe how Salat-ul-Jumu'ah (Friday prayers) are observed. (8 marks)**

A general description of Salat would gain some credit but the question wants you to focus on the Friday procedures including the khutbah.

(b) **Explain the importance of the Imam for Muslims today. (7 marks)**

In your answer you need to fit all the things that the Imam does into an explanation of why these things are important for a Muslim community and why they are particularly relevant in today's world.

(c) **'People need to have set times and set routines for prayer.'**

Do you agree? Give reasons to support your opinion and show you have thought about different points of view. You must refer to Islam in your answer. (5 marks)

The discussion is likely to include points about the danger of routine becoming habit and losing its meaning. Do not forget to refer to prayer in Islam. Consider the Muslim attitude to the value of regular repetition in worship. You may wish to consider the matter of set times separately from set ways of worship.

4 (a) When Muslims build a mosque, which religious features are essential and what is their purpose? (*8 marks*)

The question wants you to select the main features in a mosque and describe what they are for. The main requirements for prayer are that a Muslim should pray in a clean place and facing Makkah. What features are most needed by these Muslims in their mosque? Are there any other essential items even if they are not the most important religious features?

(b) Explain the importance of the mosque for a Muslim community. (*7 marks*)

The main importance of the mosque is that it is the place of prostration. Consider all the other functions of a mosque and explain why these are important for the community. You may wish to include the importance of the mosque for Muslims in a non-Muslim country.

(c) 'There is no need to go to a special building; you can pray to God anywhere.'
Do you agree? Give reasons to support your opinion and show you have thought about different points of view. You must refer to Islam in your answer. (*5 marks*)

If you do agree, then think of reasons to support your point of view. You may do this at the beginning or you may wish to put your opinion at the conclusion of the discussion. If you do not agree, think of reasons other people might give who would agree. Consider how far Muslim teaching supports the statement. Give evidence from what you know about Islam. What other points of view might there be? Some people may argue about part of the sentence but not about the rest.

6

RELIGION IN THE COMMUNITY AND THE FAMILY

The following aspects of Islam: zakah (purification of wealth by payment of annual welfare due) which contributes to the welfare of the local, national and international community; birth rites and the nurture of the young; the marriage ceremony; the role of the family; funeral rites, and beliefs about death and dying, life after death.

Ye are the best of Peoples, evolved for mankind, enjoining what is right, forbidding what is wrong, and believing in Allah.

(Surah 3:110)

The Muslim calendar is dated from a very significant event called the Hijrah. This was the day when the Ummah, the Muslim community, was formed when Muhammad ﷺ and his followers migrated from Makkah to the town of al-Madinah in 622 CE. The Hijrah, the migration, was a difficult and dangerous journey but Muhammad ﷺ knew it would be worth it if he and his followers could form a society based on a common set of beliefs and values. Islam is a complete way of life and the Ummah is the worldwide community of Muslims: the nation of Islam.

Thus We have made of you an Ummah justly balanced; that ye might be witnesses over the nations.

(Surah 2:143)

ZAKAH

Muslims must show obedience to the commands known as the Five Pillars. Zakah is one of the Five Pillars. It is, therefore, obligatory. That means it is an act of 'ibadah, duty and worship, and every Muslim must do it. All Muslims are obliged to give $2\frac{1}{2}$ per cent of their residual wealth such as savings which they have received for one complete lunar year, to the needy and for community projects. This is after they have taken care of their families. A person does not pay zakah unless his or her wealth is above a certain minimum amount known as nisab.

And be steadfast in prayer and regular in charity ... for Allah sees well all that ye do. (Surah 2:110)

So establish regular Prayer and give regular Charity; and obey the Messenger, that ye may receive mercy. (Surah 24:56)

Zakah is often translated in English as 'charity', 'alms', 'welfare', 'tax', but these words do not do justice to the Arabic word nor to the meaning of this sacred practice.

The Arabic word 'zakah' means purity but it is not a cold word. It implies wholesomeness and blessing with a potential for growth, ripening, developing and bearing fruit.

Zakah is a duty but a joyful duty. Muslims believe that everything which they possess has been given to them by Allah in trust. They are not the owners; they are stewards. Zakat is not to be seen as a tax on wealth. It is not something to be avoided if possible and begrudged. Zakah is a means of purifying the remainder of their possessions and a way of purifying themselves from greed and selfishness. It stops them loving money and being materialistic. It reminds them that they should be willing to sacrifice everything for their faith if Allah commands it.

Zakah is a form of worship and should be given with sincere intention and in gratitude for being in a position to give to others. It is another way of showing submission to Allah and being part of the ummah, the worldwide Muslim community. Giving should be done with humility. This is not an occasion for boasting. It is said that it should be so secret that the left hand should not know what the right hand is doing. The exception to this would be when the giver is setting an example to encourage others to donate.

For the poor, zakah is not charity. It is the right of the poor as members of the Muslim community to receive assistance. It purifies them, also, because it frees them from the temptation to be jealous and resentful. They should not feel embarrassed about being the recipients of welfare contributions. In accepting zakah they, too, are worshipping Allah and accepting the wisdom of the will of Allah.

Zakah, in fact, gives them the chance to do something to help the rich. The poor are helping their benefactors to store up true riches.

> *It is He Who hath made you (His) agents, inheritors of the earth: He hath raised you in ranks, some above others: that He may try you in the gifts He hath given you.*
>
> (Surah 6:165)

For the Ummah, zakah is a form of social welfare and a means of ensuring a fair redistribution of income.

IN YOUR NOTES

What do these words mean to you?
- Charity
- Sacrifice
- Value

Zakah demonstrates Muslim unity as clearly as when lines of Muslims pray shoulder to shoulder or surge in vast numbers on the Hajj.

Zakah is part of the economic system. Hoarding is forbidden in Islam. Wealth is to be circulated because then everybody benefits. Making money by charging interest is forbidden so Muslims do not lend, borrow or invest money at interest.

It was the greedy selfishness of the merchants in Makkah and their lack of concern for the poor that provoked Muhammad ﷺ to want to change the economic systems of his community. From the very beginning, he saw the practical, material world as part of Allah's creation and tried to combine spiritual ideals with daily living in the Islamic community. The move to al-Madinah gave him the opportunity to work out the principles and rules for a fairer society. The new community had many practical problems, including the need to support the followers who had left everything, home and property, to follow Muhammad ﷺ to al-Madinah.

Muslims tend to regard the rules for zakah as sensible and reasonable. The fact that it is a proportion of the wealth of a Muslim means that the rich pay more than the less well off. There is a cut off point so the poor, who need every single thing they have in order to raise their families, pay nothing at all.

CALCULATING AND COLLECTING ZAKAH

The rules about how much to pay for zakah can be quite complicated though in general it is said to be $2\frac{1}{2}$ per cent (one-fortieth) when paid on money and savings. For produce from the land, Muslims pay 10 per cent if the land is irrigated naturally and only 5 per cent if it is irrigated by hand or by machinery. They also tend to pay after the harvest of the crops.

Livestock is calculated using a detailed chart but the following gives the general idea. For cattle, the rate is one one-year old for every 30 animals; for goats and sheep, one in every 40 and for every five camels a sheep or a goat is the payment. Beyond these numbers, there are further details about the number, age and gender of the animals to be given.

Precious metals are calculated at 7½ per cent but an exception is made for jewellery that is worn regularly, such as some rings. Mining produce, such as coal and oil, is reckoned at 20 per cent.

If a Muslim owns buildings that are rented out, payment should be based on 2½ per cent of the net income after paying for repairs etc. If the property is sold, the payment is based on the whole value of the property.

It is important to understand that zakah is paid on the net balance; the excess after all essential bills have been paid. Personal expenses, family allowances and other necessary expenditure are paid first before the zakah sum is worked out. This is fair and reasonable in the opinion of most Muslims. Islam is not against people having money and property and it is realistic enough to realise that trying to make everyone economically equal is not likely to work.

Zakah is not paid on an unexpected gift but some Shi'ah Muslims pay 20 per cent of such money to their religious leaders. This is known as khums (a fifth) but is not zakah. This surprise asset would not be gained from something like a lottery win because Muslims do not believe in gambling for the obvious reasons that it can become addictive, it can be a waste of money and it encourages people to be envious and to want something for nothing.

If a Muslim lends money (without interest of course) the loan is still part of the lender's own assets and should be included in assessment for zakah.

According to Islamic law Muslim countries have the authority to collect and distribute zakah as in the days of the Prophet and of the Kalifahs. Some Muslim states tend to follow this practice but others leave the payment to the conscience of the person. Saudi Arabia is an example of a country where the Government collects zakah as normal income tax and

THINKING POINTS

- The Qur'an often links prayer and giving zakat. Why might this be?
- Why is charging interest forbidden in Islam?
- When you give something away, you become richer. Is this true?
- In the Western world, lottery money is used to fund all sorts of charitable causes. Do you think this fact should lead Muslims in the West to change their attitude to the lottery?

it is used by the state for social services. It ensures that food, clothing, housing, medicine and education can be provided for every person.

In the United Kingdom, as in other non-Muslim countries, zakah is left to the conscience of the individual Muslim and is usually done through the arrangements at the local mosque.

The money cannot be used for the upkeep of the mosque because that would be like spending it on oneself, so it will be distributed to help the needy locally or sent to Muslim aid organisations. Sometimes Muslims send the contribution abroad to relatives to give to a worthy Muslim cause in another country.

In non-Muslim countries Muslims must also pay their taxes to the government, but tax laws in many

A zakat box outside a mosque

western countries allow deductions for people who have covenanted money to charity. In Britain, ordinary banks help Muslim clients by arranging for any interest earned to be channelled directly into chosen charities.

Zakah is paid annually each lunar year. A special blessing from Allah is received by those who give to the poor during Ramadan, the month of fasting, so Muslims often give the annual contribution just before the festival of Id-ul-Fitr when the fast is finishing. Some give an additional payment at this time, called Zakat-ul-Fitr, because fasting makes Muslims feel a sense of identity and solidarity with the poor. The local mosque will suggest how much is appropriate; for example, that each family pays the equivalent of the cost of a meal for each member of the family.

For zakah, $2\frac{1}{2}$ half per cent is only the minimum to be donated. Muslims may offer more if they wish and they can make *sadaqah*, voluntary contributions, at any time they wish to do so; for example, when there is an appeal during a disaster such as a flood.

> *And spend your substance in the cause of Allah ... do good; for Allah loveth those who do good.*
>
> (Surah 2:195)

Sadaqah does not only mean giving money. It can involve giving time, talents, prayer, sympathy and a cheery smile. Any helpful deed counts, whether to a Muslim or a non-Muslim.

Muslims do not regard zakah as a burden. There would be no point in begrudging the contributions that need to be made.

> *By no means shall ye attain righteousness unless ye give (freely) of that which ye love; and whatever ye give, of a truth Allah knoweth it well.*
>
> (Surah 3:92)

> *The generous man is near Allah, near Paradise, near men and far from Hell, and the ignorant man who is generous is dearer to Allah than a worshipper who is miserly.*
>
> (Hadith)

It would be pointless trying to cheat because Allah sees everything and Muslims know they will have to answer to Allah on the Day of Judgement when the record of their deeds will show if they have been generous and honest. Not paying the true amount would be stealing from the poor and from Allah.

> *Those who believe, and do deeds of righteousness, and establish regular prayers and regular charity, will have their reward with their Lord.*
>
> (Surah 2:277)

WHO RECEIVES ZAKAH?

Trying to calculate zakah fairly may be complicated but so is distributing it.

The Qur'an lists the eight categories of people who should receive zakah:

> *Alms are for*
>   *the poor*
>   *and the needy,*
>   *and those employed to administer the (funds);*
>   *for those whose hearts have been (recently)*
>   *reconciled (to Truth);*
>   *for those in bondage*
>   *and in debt;*
>   *in the cause of Allah;*
>   *and for the wayfarer:*
> *(thus is it) ordained by Allah, and Allah is full of knowledge and wisdom.*
>
> (Surah 9:60)

Priority is given to relatives who fall into these categories.

FOR DISCUSSION

Suggest examples of the categories above and the ways the welfare funds might be made most useful.

ICT FOR RESEARCH

www.irw.org Find out about the work of Muslim aid organisations, including Muslim Aid, Islamic Relief and The Red Crescent.

Allah is compassionate and to carry out Allah's work on earth Muslims must show compassion.

He is not a believer who eats his fill while his neighbour remains hungry by his side. (Hadith)

Muslims feel themselves to be part of the ummah. They help or are helped by other Muslims worldwide.

As Islam spreads and as Muslims set up communities in many different countries, new challenges meet them. They turn to the Qur'an and the Sunnah and apply the principles in a changing world. Many Muslims see that zakah is a means by which Allah has taught them to care for the whole of His creation and that includes being trustworthy stewards of the environment. They also see that collective action is needed and they work alongside members of other faiths. (See pages 5 and 18, The Assisi and Ohito Declarations.)

BIRTH RITES AND THE NURTURE OF THE YOUNG

Islam teaches that Allah created the world and everything in it. At the same time, Allah cares for every individual, however poor, however small.

To Muslims, every child is a gift from Allah and to have a large number of children is a sign of Allah's blessing.

When a child is born into a Muslim family, the *Adhan* (call to prayer) is whispered in Arabic into the right ear of the baby and some parents may also say the *'Iqamah* (the command to rise and worship) into the left ear. This means that the first words the baby hears are: *'Allahu Akbar', 'Allah is the greatest'* and so it is a very significant ritual. In Britain this celebration often happens in the maternity unit of a hospital, after the baby is bathed. The words are recited usually by the oldest male present, who may be the grandfather, the father or the imam, but they can be said by a Muslim woman.

There are other customs which are observed at the birth of a baby but some are cultural traditions rather than specifically Muslim birth rites. *Tahnik* where sugar, honey or a squashed date is rubbed on the baby's gums by an elderly relative was a custom of the Prophet Muhammad ﷺ.

Seven days later there is a second significant Muslim birth rite. This is the *aqiqa* ceremony at which the father announces the name of the child to friends and relatives. The parents or the grandparents choose the name.

This is of religious significance in that the baby is being welcomed into the ummah, the worldwide family of Islam. Prayers are recited for Allah's blessing and the child's future health, prosperity and spiritual growth. The baby's head is wiped over with olive oil, then washed or shaved. Islam teaches that all babies are born free from sin so this ceremony has nothing to do with washing away sins. For some Muslims, however, the shaving is symbolic of removing all misfortune and for others it is a symbol of purity because hair is seen as unclean in some cultures. To celebrate the birth with the whole community, the equivalent weight of the shaven hair, in gold or silver, is given to the poor. Even if the baby is bald, money is given because it is seen as the new baby's first act of charity towards others as well as one way of the parents saying thank you to Allah for the gift of a child.

As in other religions, the main feature of the ceremony is the naming of the child and there is enormous significance placed on names. Muslims may name children after the Prophet or one of his family. For example, girls may be called Ayesha after one of the wives of Muhammad ﷺ or Fatimah after his daughter. Muslims may give the children names which reflect the 99 beautiful names of Allah. Abd means 'servant', and it is a common prefix to Muslim names. Islam teaches that all people are equal so no child will ever be named slave of another human being, but names expressing servitude to Allah are very appropriate for children who will be brought up to submit to their creator. Abdullah means 'servant of Allah', Abdur Rahman means 'servant of the Merciful', and Salim means 'peace'. Sometimes parents change their own names to become Abu (father of) or Umm (mother of) the child which has been born. Muhammad ﷺ is said to be the most popular name in the world at the present time. At the Aqiqa ceremony, babies are often given second names to help identify them as individuals.

FOR DISCUSSION

- Why do religions consider names to be important?
- Do you think names are important?
- Do you know any people who have changed their names and the reasons they did so?

Some Muslims offer a sacrifice after naming the child. This is a pre-Islamic tradition. One sheep or goat is offered for a girl and two animals are offered if a boy has been born. Though Muhammad ﷺ tried to protect females and make social conditions better for them, this custom reflects the fact that in many cultures and religions, a boy is a special blessing because he will be able to provide for his parents when they grow old, whilst the girls will have commitments to the families into which they have married. In Islam the family line is maintained by the boy.

Sharing food is a common way of celebrating a happy occasion and, as usual in Islam, the animal will have been slaughtered by a Halal butcher so that the meat is ritually clean, and the food will be distributed with one third for the immediate family, one third for relatives, friends and visitors and one third for the poor.

All male Muslim boys must be circumcised. It is a simple operation involving cutting off the foreskin of the penis. This rite was begun by Ibrahim and is practised also by Jews. The purpose was probably originally connected with hygiene but the rite has become a significant religious symbol; a physical mark of a spiritual commitment.

The *khitan*, circumcision, may be performed at the aqiqa ceremony or at 21 days or even later. It can be done any time up to the tenth birthday and some communities, for example, in Turkey, have a special celebration when the boy is between seven and ten years of age.

There is one other ceremony which is significant for Muslim children. This is the *Bismillah* ceremony and it is the beginning of the religious education of the child. It takes place when the child is four years old and in some places it is exactly when the child is four years, four months and four days. The child must be able to recite the first words of the Qur'an by heart. *'Bismillah ir Rahman ir Rahim', 'In the name of Allah, Most Gracious, Most Merciful.'* These are the words which begin every surah of the Qur'an except for Surah 9.

The Bismillah ceremony is a very happy and proud time for the child who is dressed in new clothes, with head covered and with the Qur'an on a stand in front of him or her. The ceremony also celebrates the first appearance of Jibril to Muhammad ﷺ and so the words of Surah 96 may be read and the child repeats them: *'Proclaim! (or Read!) in the name of thy Lord and Cherisher…'*

The madrassah

There is an hadith which says that when Muhammad ﷺ was asked about the rights of children, the Prophet replied, 'The father will give a good name and arrange a proper upbringing and education for his children'. After the initial teaching in the family, the religious education of the child continues in school. In Muslim countries, the education in the schools is Islamic but in non-Muslim countries, the children attend the *madrassah* for a few hours most evenings after school. Muslim children are taught to read Arabic so they can recite the Qur'an in the original language. They will learn the calligraphy and about the history of Islam and the rules of the faith. The child will learn what is *fard*, obligatory, what is *halal*, permitted, and what is *haram*, forbidden. A Muslim's whole life is governed by *Shari'ah*, the straight path, which is based on the Qur'an and the Sunnah.

By the age of seven the child will be able to take part in the five daily prayers and, by the age of ten, to fast, though not for the whole month of Ramadan. By the age of twelve Muslims are usually considered old enough to be responsible for their own religious activities.

THE MARRIAGE CEREMONY

And among His Signs is this, that He created for you mates from among yourselves, that ye may dwell in tranquillity with them, and He has put love and mercy between your (hearts): verily, in that are Signs for those who reflect.

(Surah 30:21)

Marriages in the Muslim community are often arranged marriages but they only take place with the consent of both parties. All Muslims are expected to marry and the age at which they do so depends on the civil law operating in the country in which the Muslims are living. Muslims may have up to four wives but each wife must be treated equally.

... marry women of your choice, two, or three, or four; but if ye fear that ye shall not be able to deal justly (with them), then only one

(Surah 4:3)

The existing wives must give their consent before the Muslim may take another wife. Muhammad ﷺ had many wives. Some say he had fourteen. Nine of his wives outlived him.

In actual fact, in modern times, many Muslims only have one wife because of the laws of the country in which they live. A Muslim man may marry a Jew or a Christian, but a Muslim woman may only marry a Muslim man. Divorce is allowed in Islam though it is regarded as a last resort.

A Muslim marriage usually takes place in the home or the mosque. The couple give their consent before a minimum of two witnesses.

During the ceremony, there are readings from the Qur'an. Surah 4 is often used.

O mankind! Reverence your Guardian-Lord, who created you from a single Person, created, of like nature, his mate, and from them twain scattered (like seeds) countless men and women — reverence Allah, through Whom ye demand your mutual (rights), and (reverence) the wombs (that bore you): for Allah ever watches over you.

(Surah 4:1)

The imam is likely to pray for the couple and so will the guests. In their prayers, they wish such things as material blessings, long life and many children.

The *Aqd Nikah* (contract of marriage) is spoken as well as written. The bride and groom sometimes sign up to three copies of this. This is to ensure that the bride and the groom have each consented to the union.

The groom gives *mahr* (a sum of money), some property or another valuable gift to the bride and this remains her property for life. Sunni Muslims have slightly different arrangements from Shi'ah Muslims about the giving of the bridal money. Shi'ah Muslims give mahr immediately, whereas some Sunni Muslims arrange to give part of the endowment at a later time.

There will be refreshments and celebrations after the contract is agreed but these, like the dress, decor and entertainment, will follow local customs rather than any specifically Muslim traditions. Often there is a *walimah*, which is a wedding feast.

Sometimes the bride does not actually attend the ceremony. She may remain at home while the bridegroom goes to the mosque, and she appoints an agent and two witnesses to represent her part of the contract. They hear her affirm three times at home that she is willing to be married and they speak for her during the ceremony. In the United Kingdom, to comply with the law of the land, there will be a civil wedding in front of the registrar as well as the religious ceremony.

STUDY THIS PASSAGE

And say to the believing women that they should lower their gaze and guard their modesty; that they should not display their beauty and ornaments except what (must ordinarily) appear thereof; that they should draw their veils over their bosoms and not display their beauty except to their husbands, their fathers, their husbands' fathers, their sons, their husbands' sons, their brothers or their brothers' sons, or their sisters' sons, or their women, or the slaves whom their right hands possess, or male servants free from physical needs, or small children who have no sense of the shame of sex; and that they should not strike their feet in order to draw attention to their hidden ornaments. And O ye Believers! Turn ye all together towards Allah, that ye may attain Bliss.

THE ROLE OF THE FAMILY

Marriage in Islam is more than the union of the bride and the groom; it is the uniting of two families. It is usual for the wife to live with the husband's family. Most Muslim families are extended families, even in the United Kingdom, rather than the small nuclear families which are common in western society nowadays. Other relatives who do not live in the same house may live very close nearby and children will grow up surrounded by grandparents, aunts, uncles and other members of the family.

Marriage and family life are very important in Islam. Traditionally the man's duty is to go out to work to support the family and the woman's duty is to bring up the children and look after the house. The father makes the main decisions whilst the mother is important within the home and must be shown respect by her husband and children. This is seen as the natural order of things and the way that Allah intended men and women to live.

A woman must protect her husband's property; she must be faithful to him and she must dress modestly and cover herself when in the presence of people outside the family or when she goes outside the home.

The word *hijab* means 'veil' and is used both for the scarf and for the modest clothes which most Muslim women wear in order not to tempt men and in order to preserve their own dignity. Both Muslim men and Muslim women may be shocked by the clothing worn by girls and women in western secular society. Skimpy clothes and western fashions are often seen by Muslims not as the exercise of personal choice and freedom but as the exploitation of women by men and by the media. Of course, in the United Kingdom, some Muslim young women and girls sometimes wish to dress like their peer group and this can cause arguments in the home.

This bride has patterns drawn in henna on her hands.

Muslim women and girls who wish to observe the rules of Islam often find there are less problems than in the past because schools and places of work in the West have become more accommodating in their dress codes.

Muslim girls keep their arms and legs covered for PE and games at school

The issue of women's clothes is more complicated than it looks on the surface. It is relevant to some other matters concerning women's rights in the modern world.

In some Muslim countries, women have not been educated and are treated almost as servants so the clothing is seen as a mark of servitude. In other Muslim countries, some educated women have chosen to revert to wearing traditional garb, using it as a symbol to disassociate themselves from what they see as a corrupting western influence. These women have done this by choice but they would not be willing to do so if wearing traditional clothes was made compulsory. When women are made to wear traditional clothes against their will and punished by individuals or by society for disobedience, then the issue has become one of human rights.

Muhammad ﷺ tried to make conditions better for the downtrodden, including women. From the time of Muhammad ﷺ, Muslim women have had the right to own property. They can inherit wealth although only half as much as a male relative. This is because men have dependants but women are not responsible for their male relatives.

Women are equal before Allah. They may attend mosque but they have separate washing facilities and usually perform salah in a separate area, often behind the men. This is to avoid distracting the men from their worship, but also for the benefit of the women. It is considered to

When women are covered totally, they are said to be in purdah. This is a custom in some countries. The black chador gives complete privacy.

be a respectful and thoughtful arrangement, so that they can keep their dignity when prostrating before Allah. Women are expected to take part in Friday communal prayers at noon but they usually do this at home because it is understood by males and females alike that their role is to put the family's needs first. Women are allowed to work if they can do so without neglecting their family.

Men also are expected to show modesty and restraint. They, also, should be faithful and not indulge in sex outside marriage. The Qur'an says that *'Men are the protectors and maintainers of women, because Allah has given the one more (strength) than the other, and because they support them from their means.'* (Surah 4:34). Providing for a family is a great responsibility.

> ### THINKING POINT
>
> In many cultures it has been traditional to regard women as more impulsive and irrational than men and to assume that women are ruled by their emotions and that they are more interested in relationships than in matters such as politics and world affairs. How common is this attitude today and what do you think about the roles of men and women?

THE ELDERLY

One significant point about Muslim family life is the respect given to the elderly in the extended family and the protection afforded to those on the fringe of family life, single relatives, who might otherwise be very lonely or neglected.

> *Thy Lord hath decreed that ye worship none but Him, and that ye be kind to parents. Whether one or both of them attain old age in thy life, say not to them a word of contempt, nor repel them, but address them in terms of honour. And, out of kindness, lower to them the wing of humility, and say: 'My Lord! Bestow on them thy Mercy even as they cherished me in childhood.*
>
> (Surah 17:23–24).

Muslims very rarely put their parents in old folks' homes. The old are treated with respect and their experience is regarded as a valuable asset for the whole family. Often the elderly find they have a new role to play in the family in that they are helpful with the young people and provide a willing listening ear when parents may be too busy to give enough time and attention.

Mutual care and concern in the family between all the members is seen as a reflection of Allah's compassion and a way of showing gratitude for his love.

FUNERAL RITES

When Muslims hear of a death they say, *'To Allah we belong, and to Him is our return—'* (Surah 2:156). This shows that they hope the person will be claimed by Allah to live in Paradise.

The funeral rites for Muslims are not found in the Qur'an but in law books, so there may be differences in the way these are observed. Rituals also vary according to the customs of the country. In the United Kingdom, local authorities differ in the provision they make for Muslim funerals. Some areas have separate burial plots in their cemeteries for Muslims and the graves run from northeast to southwest, so the heads can be at the southwest end facing right, towards the direction of Makkah and the Ka'bah.

It is important to Muslims that the dead are buried and not cremated. Cremation is not allowed. This is in common with Jews and many Christians who have similar beliefs in that they want the bodies to be intact for the resurrection of the dead from their graves at the Day of Judgement.

When Muslims are dying, they say the words which Muhammad is reported to have said, *'Allah, help me through the hardship and agony of death'*. Like the Prophet, they pray for forgiveness and they also repeat the *Shahadah* (declaration of faith): *'There is no god but Allah; Muhammad is the messenger of Allah'*. Thus the last word heard by a Muslim is the same word heard at birth: the name of God, Allah. Relatives recite verses from the Qur'an to invoke the *barakah* (grace) of Allah and they repeat loudly, *'La ilaha illal lahu', 'There is no god but Allah'*, to reinforce the concentration of the dying person on this *kalimah* (statement of faith) so that Shaytan (the devil) will have no opportunity to confuse the believer with doubts.

Girls learning how to perform a Muslim burial

The dead body is placed on a stretcher with the head in the direction of the *qiblah* ready for the *ghusl*, a ritual washing, carried out by relatives of the same sex as the deceased. The limbs are straightened then the corpse is washed three times, perfumed with scents such as camphor, wrapped in a shroud, a single piece of unsewn cloth, and placed in a coffin.

The body of a Muslim is carried to the grave by the family

Sometimes the cloths worn on the Hajj pilgrimage to Makkah are used; three for a man and five for a woman, and they have been dipped in water brought from the Zamzam well. Martyrs, killed in a jihad, are buried unwashed so their blood is still witness to their fate. Ideally they are buried where they fell.

All bodies should be buried in contact with the earth. Laws in many countries require coffins but in some Muslim countries the body is placed straight into the ground, protected by planks of wood or with the coffin inverted over it and then covered with earth. Salat is performed in the house of the dead Muslim or in the mosque.

The body is carried as a sign of respect, rather than transported by vehicle, to the cemetery by a procession of male Muslims.

The funeral takes place as soon as possible, preferably the next day, but certainly within three days. In hot countries this is very important, but even in the United Kingdom some Muslims prefer to send the dead by aeroplane to Pakistan or India. This is purely for sentimental reasons.

At the graveside in the cemetery, funeral prayers Salat-ul-Janaza (which is salah with no prostrations), and al-Fatihah (Surah 1) (see page 4) are said. Al-Fatihah is a very important statement of belief in Allah and his mercy.

Muslims are buried with the head turned to face Makkah. As the corpse is lowered into the ground, the body is committed to the earth with the words, *'In the name of Allah, (we bury) according to the Way of the Prophet of Allah'*, and the following is also said: *'From the (earth) did We create you, and into it shall We return you, and from it shall We bring you out once again.'* (Surah 20:55). These words show the belief that Allah will take the dead to Paradise at the Day of Judgement. Prayers include petitions for forgiveness for all, the living and the dead, and for the mourners to be kept faithful. Seven days after the burial, relatives often visit the grave of the deceased as a mark of respect.

The expression of grief is acceptable, but there should not be excessive lamentation, wailing and mourning. Death is a sad event but it is normal and

ICT FOR RESEARCH

See the visually enhanced panoramic view of the Taj Mahal at Agra in Encarta.

The Taj Mahal, built in the seventeenth century CE in India, is considered to be one of the finest examples of Islamic architecture. It is in fact a mausoleum which contains the tombs of Mumtaz Mahal and the emperor Shah Jahan, her husband.

believers should accept this fact with faith and trust. Muhammad ﷺ wept when his son died and Muslims regard it as natural for men, as well as for women, to show their feelings at such a time. The sadness of separation from the loved one is tinged with happiness at the knowledge that the will of Allah is for the best. According to the Qur'an, those who believe and live by their beliefs need have no fear of death nor should they grieve excessively. In some communities, it is thought that mourning should not last more than three days. Some limit it to a week but there are others where it is traditional to remember the dead for up to three months. An exception is usually made for widows to allow them to mourn for longer; some may mourn for four months and ten days. They should not remarry during that time. Muslims make sure that mourners are not left alone during their time of mourning. They console the members of the family, helping them to come to terms with their loss and reminding them, yet again, of the important lesson: that all human beings belong to Allah and all eventually have to return to Him.

When they call to pay their respects after a bereavement, visitors bring their own food so they are not a burden on the mourners.

Shi'ah Muslims have some different traditions including *rawdahs* which are memorial gatherings on the fortieth day of mourning. They also have more elaborate tombs. This is probably the result of cultural influence from the East from the times when Islam was ruled from Damascus by the Ummayyad dynasty and then from Baghdad by the Abbasid dynasty.

There are not supposed to be impressive monuments in a Muslim cemetery; rich and poor are alike in death. The name of the person is the only decoration needed. Many Muslims consider that donations should be given to the poor rather than spending money on extravagant tombstones. It is traditional for the grave to be raised a little above the level of the ground but this is simply to stop people from walking on it or sitting on it.

Funeral prayers at the graveside

BELIEFS ABOUT DEATH AND DYING

Life does not finish when we die, according to Islam. Death is a stage of life not the end of it. The real permanent life is *akhirah*, life after death; eternal life, everlasting life. Muslims do not believe in reincarnation. There is only the one life on earth for each person. In this one life we can each work for success in the never-ending life. There is no second chance. There will be a test on the Day of Judgement (Surahs 81 and 82) when all our actions will be judged by Allah. Those who succeed will be rewarded by Paradise (*al-Jannah*), a place of permanent happiness and joy, and those who fail will suffer in Hell (*Jahannam*) which is a place of eternal torment and pain.

> *Then those who have believed and worked righteous deeds shall be made happy in a Mead of Delight. And those who have rejected Faith and falsely denied Our Signs and the meeting of the Hereafter, — such shall be brought forth to punishment.*
>
> (Surah 30:15–16).

Muslims believe that at death two angels of justice, Munkar and Nakir, visit the person and record their good deeds and their bad deeds to see if they are fit to enter Paradise. The angels ask questions such as, 'Who is your God?', 'What is your religion?' and 'Who is your prophet?' Mourners at the graveside try to encourage the deceased person to give suitable answers.

As the mourners walk from the grave it is often the practice to turn and recite the Kalimah again.

Muslims believe that until the Day of Judgement, Azra'il, the angel of death, takes the dead to *barzakh*, a sort of limbo, outside of time, where they will await the last day.

AKHIRAH, LIFE AFTER DEATH

At the Day of Judgement, Muslims believe there will be a complete physical resurrection of the body. Allah will have no difficulty in putting these dead bodies back together, including their fingerprints:

> *Does man think that We cannot assemble his bones? Nay, We are able to put together in perfect order the very tips of his fingers.*
>
> (Surah 75:3–4)

The Day of Judgement is obviously very important for Muslims. It is also known, among many other names, as:

The Day of Requital, the Day of Reckoning, the Day of Meeting, the Day of Gathering Together, the Day of Abiding, the Day of Coming Out and the Day of Mutual Loss and Gain.

The Qur'an describes the end of the world vividly, e.g. Surahs 81 and 82. Stars will scatter, mountains will tumble, oceans will boil over, the dead will be raised from their tombs and everyone will be judged.

The good deeds will be balanced against the bad. Intentions are also taken into account. In an Hadith it says that a good intention counts as a good deed and if it is carried out the good deed is recorded as ten good deeds. If a person intended to do a bad deed but then relented and did not do it, Allah in his mercy counts this as a good deed. If the person goes ahead and commits the bad deed, it is still only one bad deed.

If the good deeds outweigh the bad, the person will go to Paradise; if the bad deeds outweigh the good, the person will go to Hell. Muslims believe that after punishment some people may be allowed into Paradise but not if they have committed something really wicked such as *shirk*, the sin of believing in something other than Allah.

Though the end of the world is described very dramatically, the rewards and punishments of the afterlife are generally considered by Muslims to be symbolic picture language. Eternal life is beyond human imagining. It is a whole new dimension of existence. Even family relationships will change beyond earthly experience.

> *Then when the Trumpet is blown, there will be no more relationships between them that day nor will one ask after another!*
>
> (Surah 23:101)
>
> *We have decreed Death to be your common lot, and We are not to be frustrated from changing your Forms and creating you (again) in (forms) that ye know not.*
>
> (Surah 56:60–61)

Symbolic descriptions of Paradise in Surah 37:42–45 tell of *'Fruits (delights)… in Gardens of Felicity, Thrones and Fountains, clear-flowing and delicious to those who drink.'* Other descriptions tell of flowers and birds, of fruit served by youths and maidens, of soft couches, silken cushions, goblets and dishes fashioned in gold and of *'all that the souls could desire and the eyes delight in'*.

The symbolic description of punishment in Jahannam, the place of blazing hellfire under the earth, is described equally graphically but in blood-curdling imagery of torture in black smoke and boiling water.

Muslims believe that the Judgement is not because Allah is some sort of cruel tyrant. The fate of people is inevitable because it results from their own actions.

> *Therefore do I warn you of a Fire blazing fiercely; none shall reach it but those most unfortunate ones Who gave the lie to Truth and turn their backs. But those most devoted to Allah shall be removed far from it—*
>
> (Surah 92:14–17)

PRACTICE EXAMINATION QUESTIONS

1 (a) Describe how Muslims give zakah and how it is used. (*8 marks*)

   The description of how it is given and distributed should be quite detailed.

   (b) Explain why zakah is important both for individual Muslims and for the ummah as a whole. (*7 marks*)

   Explain why zakah helps the givers as well as the recipients and the value this has for the unity of ummah.

   (c) 'Helping the poor is the most important religious practice.'

   Do you agree? Give reasons to support your opinion and show you have thought about different points of view. You must refer to Islam in your answer. (*5 marks*)

   Remember to refer to Islam and to pay attention to the word 'most'.

2 (a) Describe the ceremonies which take place at the start of a Muslim baby's life. (*8 marks*)

   Good responses to this question might begin with the adhan, the call to prayer, whispered in Arabic into the right ear of the baby and the 'iqamah, the command to rise and worship, in the left ear. The Aqiqa ceremony is essential and reference might also be made to sacrifice and circumcision because they are fairly common ceremonies.

   (b) Explain the religious meaning of these ceremonies and their importance for Muslims. (*7 marks*)

   Any symbolism should be explained along with specific meanings of ceremonies and the importance should include the significance of rites of passage in general, of ceremonies at birth for Muslims and concepts such as continuity with the past.

(c) 'It is good for children to be brought up to perform religious practices regularly.'

   Do you agree? Give reasons to support your opinion and show you have thought about different points of view. You must refer to Islam in your answer. (*5 marks*)

   There are a number of equally valid approaches to this debate. You may wish to define words such as 'good' and 'regularly' before deciding how far you agree or disagree. In Islam it is considered parental duty to bring up children in the faith. Performing religious practices out of habit is not necessarily a bad thing.

3 (a) Describe a Muslim marriage ceremony. (*8 marks*)

   The description can be of one specific ceremony or it may be a more general description which mentions that there are variable factors and concentrates on the essential parts such as the witnesses and the contract.

   (b) Explain the importance of marriage and family life for Muslims. (*7 marks*)

   This is an opportunity to show that you understand that though the marriage ceremony is more of a secular event than religious, all life is part of Allah's plan and marriage and family life are important for the spread of Islam, the worship of Allah and the good of humans. It mirrors the ummah. It is co-operative rather than competitive. Practical examples of love and care and the roles within the family will help your explanation.

   (c) 'A marriage ceremony is not an important religious ceremony for Muslims.'

   Do you agree? Give reasons to support your opinion and show you have thought about different points of view. (*5 marks*)

   Plan the answer carefully so that the information is not simply repeated but used to the greatest effect.

4 (a) Describe how the body of a Muslim is prepared for burial and buried. (*8 marks*)

Include most of the factual description found in this chapter which is relevant to this question. You have not been asked to explain the significance so do not waste time on it except where it helps to tie the factual account together.

(b) Explain how beliefs about life after death might affect the way Muslims live. (*7 marks*)

You will need to outline what Muslims believe about the Day of Judgement in order to explain the ways in which beliefs in eternal bliss in Paradise and everlasting punishment in Hell may affect the way Muslims practise the rituals of their faith but also may alter the character of the believers and their treatment of other people. Make a few notes about the effects before you begin so that you keep the actual question in mind.

(c) 'Religious people should welcome death.' Do you agree? Give reasons to support your opinion and show you have thought about different points of view. You must refer to Islam in your answer. (*5 marks*)

Consider what the range of Muslim opinion might be before you start .You may wish to point out that it all depends on certain factors before a decision could be made about the statement. Often in discussions it is not as straightforward as saying, 'yes this is true because …' or 'no this is not true because …'. Different points of view do not have to be totally opposite. They could be a discussion of the sort of factors which should be taken into consideration.

SACRED WRITINGS

Most religions in the world today have writings which are considered to be sacred by their followers. This means the writings are divinely inspired and believers can turn to them for guidance about spiritual beliefs and practical living. They are holy books and are treated with respect.

THE QUR'AN

The Muslim holy book is the Qur'an which was revealed to the prophet Muhammad ﷺ between the years 610–632 CE. The first revelation took place in the month of Ramadan 610 CE in the cave of Hira on a mountain called al-Nur.

> *That this is indeed a Qur'an most honourable, in a Book well-guarded, which none shall touch but those who are clean: a revelation from the Lord of the Worlds.*
>
> (Surah 56:77–80)

The word Qur'an means 'reading' or 'recitation' in Arabic. The book is not a collection of the words of Muhammad ﷺ. Tradition says that the Prophet could not read nor write. Muslims believe that the original Qur'an, usually called 'the mother of the book', is in heaven. The Qur'an is the words of Allah. The words were read or recited to Muhammad ﷺ by the archangel Jibril (Gabriel) at the command of Allah. Jibril's first words to Muhammad ﷺ were, *'Proclaim (or read) in the name of Allah …'*

After that dramatic and strange experience on Laylat-ul-Qadr, the Night of Power, on one of the last ten days of Ramadan in the year 610 CE, the angel communicated with Muhammad ﷺ many times. Sometimes the Prophet lay in his cloak, semi-conscious and sweating as the message came, other times he was out riding; sometimes it came clearly and directly as he was speaking and other times like a muffled bell ringing in his head.

It is said that it was twenty-two years, five months and, possibly, four days after the first revelation that the last revealed verse was given:

> *This day have I perfected for you your religion, completed My favour upon you, and have chosen Islam as your religion.*
>
> (Surah 5:3)

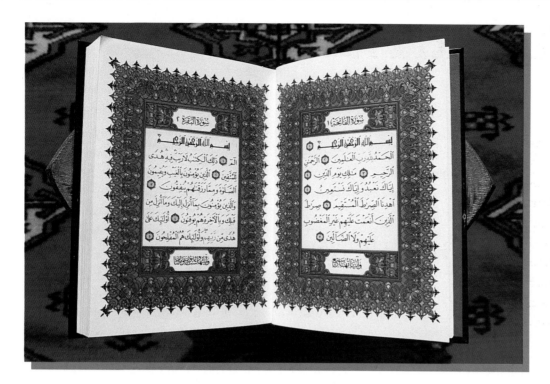

The Qur'an

In Surah 97 it says that the Qur'an came to earth in its entirety on Laylat-ul-Qadr. Muslim theologians explain that it came to a spiritual sphere above the earth called the Bayt al-Izza, the House of Glory, where eternity meets our world of time, and from there Jibril over the years imprinted it on the heart of the Prophet.

The Qur'an is in Arabic and is therefore read from right to left, starting at the top of the page. The book begins at what readers of English would consider to be the back of the book. The form of the Qur'an is not prose; it is poetry. It has rhyme and rhythm.

The Qur'an is divided into *surahs* or chapters and these are made up of verses, *ayat*. One verse or unit is an *ayah*. The word means 'a sign'.

There are over 6,000 verses in the Qur'an. The numbering of the verses is not part of the original text and though numbers are a help when referring to the sacred book, sometimes the numbers vary. The actual text is always the same. The important thing for Muslims is that not just every verse but every word and every letter comes directly from Allah.

The 114 surahs are arranged according to length with the longest chapters at the beginning and much shorter surahs at the end. The main exception is the first surah, which is short but very significant for Muslim *iman*, faith.

The name of the first surah is *al-Fatihah*, the Opening (see page 76).

Each surah has a name, taken from near the beginning of the chapter or from a distinctive word in it. The longest chapter, Surah 2, is called 'The Cow' or 'The Heifer' because verse 69 refers to 'a fawn-coloured heifer, pure and rich in tone'. The shortest is actually Surah 108 and it is called 'Abundance'. It contains only three verses:

In the name of Allah, Most Gracious, Most Merciful.
To thee have We granted the Fount (of Abundance).
Therefore to thy Lord turn in Prayer and Sacrifice. For he who hateth thee — he will be cut off (From Future Hope).

All surahs apart from Surah 9 begin with the words, *'Bismillah-ir-Rahman-ir-Rahim'*, *'In the name of Allah, Most Gracious, Most Merciful.'*

The Qur'an is divided into thirty parts and each part is known as 'juz'. These divisions are to help in the reciting; for example, they enable the whole book to be read in a month. The Qur'an is seen as a whole book, not a collection of chapters. It is a unity and is called al-kitab, the book or the scripture.

The surahs are not in the order in which they were received by Muhammad ﷺ. He memorised the Qur'an as he heard it, and then repeated everything to his followers, who learnt it and wrote it down. Towards the end of his ministry he often dictated the revelations to Zayd Bin Thabit who was his scribe or secretary. At least five of the companions of the Prophet memorised all the revelations. Muslims still try to do this today.

The Qur'an was not compiled as one book until after the death of the Prophet. Since then it has remained unchanged and Muslims say that it cannot be translated into any other language from the original Arabic because that would change the words of Allah. The Qur'an is only truly the Qur'an when it is in Arabic.

Two years after the death of Muhammad ﷺ the first Khalifah, Abu Bakr, at the advice of 'Umar, another companion of the Prophet, had all the pieces of the Qur'an collected into one book. They had been written on a variety of materials such as paper, cloth, leather, pottery, leaves of palm trees and even old bones. These pieces had been kept in a chest by Hafsa, the daughter of 'Umar. Hafsa was one of the Prophet's wives. The order of the Qur'an was told to Muhammad ﷺ by Jibril and he ensured that his followers knew the correct order of the verses.

Zayd Bin Thabit was made responsible for collecting the fragments and having them copied into one volume under the supervision of a committee. The final copy was shown to those who had memorised all of the messages and they agreed that it was accurate; it was complete and word-perfect. The book was given to Hafsa for safe keeping.

Many followers already knew some surahs of the Qur'an by heart and other written versions and part collections started to appear during the reign of 'Umar, who became the second Khalifah. In some ways this was inevitable because 'Umar had encouraged the foundation of schools for teaching the Qur'an. Islam was spreading and for some of the converts Arabic was not their first language. The third Khalifah, 'Uthman, feared that the situation might get out of hand and cause confusion. He consulted the companions of the Prophet and a committee of four was set up. It was led by Zayd. They made four copies based on the official version and sent one to each of four Islamic cities: Basra, Damascus, al-Kufa and al-Madinah. The year was 652 CE, twenty years after the Prophet's death.

Two very early copies of the Qur'an still exist and are said to be two of the original four manuscripts mentioned above. One is in Istanbul and one in Tashkent (Uzbekistan).

Damascus
al-Kufa
Basra
Persian Gulf
Red Sea
al-Madinah

FOR DISCUSSION

Is there a difference between a book being called 'the word of God' and 'the words of God'?

THE REASONS WHY THE QUR'AN IS A SACRED TEXT FOR MUSLIMS

Wahy is a word specially used by Muslims to mean 'revelation'. It is only prophets who receive a revelation. The word *rasul* means prophet. The word *risalah* means prophethood.

People can glimpse truths about Allah from his creation, the natural world, and they are born with an instinct to worship their creator but they need the special revelation which Allah by his grace communicates through his prophets. Allah is beyond human imagining and beyond human understanding except when Allah chooses to reveal himself. That is why revelation is such an important concept.

Muslims believe that human beings have never been left without a reminder that Allah is the true centre of life. Throughout history, from the time of the Prophet Adam and Hawwa (Eve), the first humans, Allah has sent revelations to help people to live according to his will. The last of these revelations was received by Muhammad ﷺ but there were earlier ones which are referred to in the Qur'an:

- The *Sahifah*, the scroll revealed to the Prophet Ibrahim (Abraham), which no longer exists.
- *Tawrah*, the Law revealed to the Prophet Musa (Moses).
- *Zabur*, the Psalms revealed to the Prophet Dawud (David), the King of Israel and Judah.
- *Injil*, the Gospel revealed to the Prophet Isa (Jesus). The Qur'an teaches that Isa was not a son of Allah but his chosen Prophet born of Mary.

Muslims believe that the versions of the Law of Moses and the Psalms which are sacred scriptures to the Jews, and also to Christians, were changed and distorted over the centuries as was the Christian gospel. Islam was not a new religion preached by the Prophet Muhammad ﷺ. It is the original religion from the beginning of time. Muhammad ﷺ was the vehicle by which the revelation was transmitted. Not only was it essential to call people back to the true iman (faith), but it was essential that the message should never be lost or corrupted. This is the reason that the sacred scripture of Islam remains in Arabic. All Muslims learn to recite the Arabic words.

Muslims refer to the Qur'an as the 'noble' or 'glorious'; its Arabic is regarded as being beyond compare.

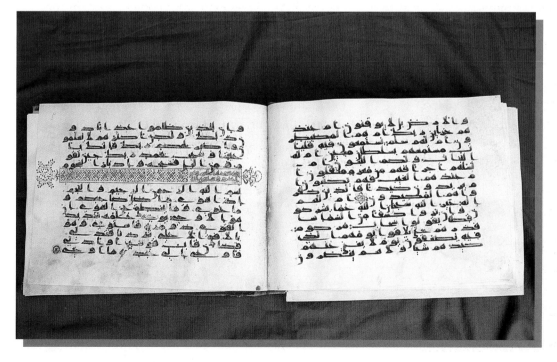

Early Qur'an written in Kufic script

Young children recite parts of the Qur'an

The earliest copies of the Qur'an were written in kufic, the most common script used for worship in the early Muslim world, and usually on vellum.

Written Arabic has only consonants so around the tenth century CE (fourth century AH) vowel signs and diacritical marks to help with pronunciation were added. There are different accepted ways of reading the Qur'an but there are no variant texts such as there are in the holy books of other religions.

The art of learning to recite with correct pronunciation is called *tajwid*. The word *qira'ah*, which is literally translated as 'reading', refers to different styles of reciting the Qur'an.
For the purpose of scholarship and study within Islam there have been commentaries on the text from early times. Learning is, for Muslims, an act of worship. *Tafsir* is the word for a commentary and the earliest main one was written by al-Tabari who died

in 923 CE. There were thirty volumes of it. Al-Baydawi (died 1286) wrote another one which is still regarded as the classic interpretation. Many Muslims would prefer the word 'interpretation' rather than commentary because there is no criticism of the text. Mostly the interpretation clarifies when in the life of Muhammad ﷺ he may have received the verse. Chapters revealed when Muhammad ﷺ was living in Makkah are known as Makki, and those revealed after the Hijrah when he was in al-Madinah are called Madani. The Makkan surahs tend to be shorter and they deal with *Tawhid* (see page 103) and the urgent need of people to turn from idolatry and to embrace the faith. The surahs from the time in al-Madinah contain details of ordering life sensibly in the new community. Between them the two groups of surahs cover all that is needed for spiritual understanding of the beliefs and for putting the faith into practice.

Muslims regard the fact that the surahs are not in chronological order as a sign of the wisdom of Allah. The Qur'an is not a history of the life of the Prophet.

ICT FOR RESEARCH

Find out about competitions for reciting the Qur'an

The revelations that he received had value to him at a particular time but in essence they are eternal.

Verse 255 of the second Surah is called *Ayat al-Kursi*, the verse of the Throne: it is about the sovereignty of Allah over the entire universe.

> *Allah! There is no god but He — the Living, the Self-subsisting, Eternal. No slumber can seize Him nor sleep. His are all things in the heavens and on earth. Who is there that can intercede in His presence except as He permitteth? He knoweth what (appeareth to His creatures as) Before or After or Behind them. Nor shall they compass aught of His knowledge except as He willeth. His Throne doth extend over the heavens and the earth, and He feeleth no fatigue in guarding and preserving them for He is the Most High, The Supreme (in glory).* (Surah 2:255)

Allah is the central theme of the Qur'an.

The basic beliefs of Islam (see Chapter 1) can be grouped into three topics:

- *Tawhid* – the oneness of Allah
- *Risalah* – prophethood
- *Akhirah* – life after death.

These are the recurring topics in the Qur'an. Readers are encouraged to submit to Allah in response to this message and to walk the straight path which will lead to peace in this life and reward in the hereafter. The Arabic sounds so beautiful to believers that many are moved to tears by the recitation of the words. Muslims believe that no human could have written it. The content, the consistency of the message and the eloquence of the Arabic make the book unique. The Qur'an itself says:

> *Or do they say, 'He forged it'? Say: 'Bring then a Surah like unto it, and call (to your aid) anyone you can, besides Allah, if it be ye speak the truth!'* (Surah 10:38)

Surah 17:88 says that if the whole of mankind and the jinns gathered together they could not produce anything like the Qur'an.

> *This Qur'an is not such as can be produced by other than Allah; on the contrary, it is a confirmation of (revelations) that went before it, and a fuller explanation of the Book—wherein there is no doubt—from the Lord of the Worlds.* (Surah 10:37)

The Qur'an provides a complete book of guidance for Muslims. It covers all aspects of human life. It is applicable at any time of history and in any part of the world. Allah revealed it and Allah preserves it.

ICT FOR RESEARCH

Look up what Encarta has to say about the Qur'an but note that the spelling is Koran.

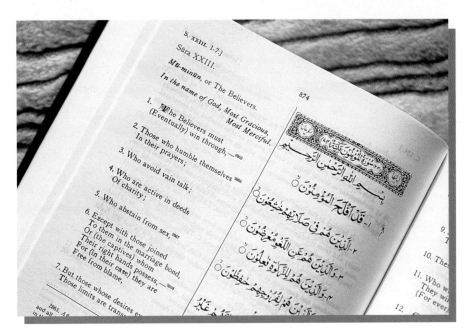

The Qur'an in Arabic and English

There are different opinions among Muslims about translating the Qur'an into other languages. Having a translation for use in worship is not really an issue.

To Muslims the fact that since the time of Muhammad ﷺ the whole ummah has continued to use the same words over the centuries and throughout the world is a fact that makes them marvel and fills them with awe. No Muslim would seriously suggest changing the language of worship.

Translations exist for other purposes rather than worship. Non-Muslim scholars have wished to read the Qur'an in the present day and similarly in the past. The Arab conquests of the seventh century influenced many cultures and Islam was the source of learning about mathematics, science, astronomy, medicine, architecture, technology and anything which did not conflict with the Islamic view of the purpose of society and the aims of life. The Qur'an was translated into Latin in 1143 CE by an Englishman Robertus Retenensis, with the help of Hermannus Dalmata. The first version in English was in 1669 CE. It was based on an earlier French version. Printing had been invented by then in the West and was an important factor in change and development.

An English or any other non-Arabic translation of the Qur'an is not the Qur'an but, all the same, mass produced copies printed in many languages seemed at first to lessen the dignity of the holy book in the eyes of some Muslims. Nowadays, however, there are text books about Islam for non-Muslim and Muslim students and Muslims themselves may read from a text of the Qur'an such as the Yusuf Ali translation where the Arabic and the English are side by side on the page.

FOR DISCUSSION

What are the points for and against holy books being translated:
- into other languages, or
- into more modern versions of the original language?

SUNNAH (HADITH)

The second source of knowledge for Muslims is the record of the sayings and doings of the Prophet. Muhammad ﷺ is regarded as the role-model for living the perfect human life so it was only natural that believers should wish to know all that he said and did. These sayings and deeds are known as the Sunnah, the trodden path, the way, or the custom and example of the Prophet. Muhammad ﷺ himself made it clear which of his actions were intended as an example and which were simply his own personal way of doing things. Biographies of the life of Muhammad ﷺ have been in existence from very early times. One *sirah* (biography) was made by Zohri Ibn Hisham who knew A'isha, the wife of Muhammad ﷺ, and a shorter version was written by a scholar who had studied under Zohri. He was Ibn Ishaq, and this version is available in an English translation.

Individual verbal traditions of what the Prophet said or did are known as hadith. The word *hadith* means a saying, news, or a report. The plural is *ahadith*.

The Qur'an is complete and unalterable but sometimes it is difficult for Muslims to be sure exactly what they should do. In the early days, there were people who had heard what Muhammad ﷺ explained as his understanding of the revelation. Salah, prayer, is a good example of this. The Qur'an tells people when to pray and to face Makkah and to wash but it does not give details of the words or the movements during prayer. Muslims simply copied what the Prophet used to do and say when he prayed.

There are two types of Hadith; the Prophetic and the Qudsi or Sacred. The Prophetic are wise sayings and advice which the Prophet gave. The Sacred sayings are ones in which Muhammad ﷺ quotes Words from Allah which are not part of the Qur'an. None of the ahadith are revelation, they do not have the status and authority of the Qur'an, but they are inspired sayings and they are treated with reverence by many Muslims. They are second in authority to the Qur'an.

Long ago, many cultures and communities relied on the spoken word and were far more used to remembering things than we are today. Mistakes might creep in but oral tradition was not like a game of Chinese Whispers where the message inevitably changes as it is passed on. Each hadith tends to include a list of credentials; a chain of narration which identifies who told whom. A typical example goes as follows:

> *On the authority of Abu Hamza Anas Iibn Malik (may Allah be pleased with him), the servant of the Messenger of Allah (may the blessings and peace of Allah be upon him) that the Prophet said, 'None of you truly believes until he wishes for his brother what he wishes for himself.' It was related by a-I Bukhari and Muslim.*
> (An-Nawawi's 'Forty Hadith').

Many sayings are traced back to the youngest widow of Muhammad ﷺ. She was A'isha the daughter of Abu Bakr and she was a scholar. The chain of credentials that guarantee the authenticity of an hadith is called the *isnad*.

As time went by the ahadith numbered hundreds, then thousands. The problem with ahadith is that there is no agreed version and some of them seem to be contradictory. A Muslim scholar, Bukhari, recognised this problem and made a list of 600,000 Hadith. He then rejected all those which did not have an isnad that traced back to the companions of Muhammad ﷺ. Others he rejected because they contradicted the principles of the Qur'an or they were unjust or simply did not make sense. Bukhari's final collection numbered 2,762. Bukhari died in 870 CE.

Ahadith can be classified as *sahih* (sound), *hasan* (adequate) or *dai'if* and *saqim* (weak and inferior). The weak and inferior ahadith cannot be used in discussions on points of law but they can be useful for general meditation and ethical and moral issues. There are six collections which Muslims tend to use as the basis of *Shari'ah*, Muslim law. These are Sahih Muslim, Sunan abu Dawud, Sunan ibn Majah, Sahih al-Bukhari, Jami' at-Tirmidhe and Sunan an-Nasa'i. Some Muslims distrust Hadith and some groups favour particular collections; for example, Shi'ah Muslims only accept ahadith where the isnad traces back to 'Ali.

WAYS IN WHICH RESPECT IS SHOWN FOR THE QUR'AN

Verses from the Qur'an not only instruct but also inspire Muslims. The Arabic is beautiful visually and colourful calligraphy is used to enhance the appearance of this beautiful gift from Allah.

When a Qur'an is written, great care is taken with the calligraphy because copying it is a religious act. The same pure text has been passed down through centuries. That fact gives some idea of the respect which is shown towards the Qur'an.

The act of reciting the Qur'an, not simply with the tongue but with the heart, soul, mind, and body is known as *tilawah*. Five times a day Muslims repeat Surah 1, al-Fatihah, in their prayers. Before touching or reading the Qur'an, Muslims ensure that they are clean and have performed wudu' or have had a complete bath. Women do not touch the Qur'an during menstruation.

The Qur'an is kept wrapped in a silk cloth on the highest shelf in the house so that nothing is above it. The cloth is to keep the book clean and free from dust. It is usually placed on a *rahal* (a low stool or stand) to be read. It must not be placed on the floor and many Muslims will not hold it below the level of the navel.

Worn out Qur'ans are never thrown away. They are buried or they are weighted down and thrown into a deep river. This is to make sure that they are safe and no disrespect can be shown to them.

When reading the Qur'an a Muslim must avoid talking, eating or drinking.

Muslims start their reading by obeying the instruction given in Surah 16:98:

> *When thou does read the Qur'an, seek Allah's protection from Satan the Rejected One.*

This encourages the Muslim not to be distracted and to read with understanding and humility.

A person who memorises the Qur'an off by heart and can recite it all is called a *hafiz*, or a *hafizah* if a female. The plural is *huffaz*. Reciting is not just a habit or a ritual, it is a religious experience every time. It is common for Muslims to move their bodies very gently while they recite the Qur'an. The rhythm of the Arabic words passes into the whole body. In the mosque, verses from the Qur'an are used for decoration and to stimulate worship. The Friday *khutbah* (sermon) explains and applies teaching from the Qur'an for the benefit of the community.

During the month of Ramadan the revelation of the Qur'an on the Night of Power is remembered and Muslims spend more time studying the sacred book especially during the last ten days of the month. They read through the thirty sections into which it is divided.

The one family occasion when the Qur'an is read through aloud is when someone dies. Relatives and friends gather to take part in the reading. They may take it in turns or they may read in unison.

Reading the Qur'an at home

Words from the Qur'an are often used as decoration in the mosque

For Muslims, the Qur'an is not only for use in public and private worship. It is a handbook for living. There is no point in reading a holy book if it does not affect a person's thinking and influence their behaviour.

The Shari'ah is the code of law for Islamic living. The word means 'straight path' and its purpose is to provide what is prayed for when reciting the Fatihah (to be shown the straight way). The two main sources for Shari'ah are the Qur'an and the Sunnah, which shows the authority of these two sources in Muslim ethics and the respect that is shown for them.

On most issues the Qur'an speaks in general terms. The Sunnah shows how Muhammad ﷺ interpreted the revelation in practice. Modern life continually raises issues which are complex and new. For such situations there are two other ways of making decisions but they are still based on the Qur'an and Hadith:

- *Ijma'* which means consensus and involves discussions by Muslim scholars who are experts in the Qur'anic teaching and in ahadith.
- *Qiyas* which are comparisons. Parallels are found in the Qur'an and Hadith. For example, the modern issue of drug abuse is seen as similar to the problems that led alcohol to be banned in the past. So the use of drugs is banned too.

For many Muslims day to day living is made easier by *Fiqh* which means 'knowledge and understanding'. It is a system of Islamic law which classifies behaviour into five categories:

- *Fard*: compulsory, e.g praying five times a day. Doing this is rewarded; not doing this is punishable.
- *Mandub*: recommended, e.g. a kind deed. This would be rewarded but omission is not punished.
- *Mubah*: allowed or permissible. These deeds are harmless in themselves and have not been forbidden.
- *Makruh*: frowned upon but not forbidden so not punished. Divorce is an example of this category.
- *Haram*: forbidden such as eating unclean foods and drinking alcohol. These deeds are punished.

In a Muslim state some of these punishable offences are against the law of the country and are punished as a crime. In non-Muslim countries some things are not against the law but are against religious principles of Muslims. When their conscience is troubling them and they are not sure what to do, Muslims turn to the Qur'an for help.

The Qur'an is *'a Guidance and a Mercy'* according to Surah 10:57. Muslims are called to Jihad. They are to strive to promote good and fight evil in everyday life. The Qur'an provides answers for a Muslim when he or she needs advice and guidance in how best each person may follow the straight path. If they approach the text prayerfully, they will find a solution or a principle from which the answer could be deduced. It also gives them comfort when times are hard.

> *We said: 'Get ye down all from here: and if, as is sure, there comes to you guidance from Me, whosoever follows My guidance, on them shall be no fear, nor shall they grieve.'*
>
> (Surah 2:38)

The Qur'an has many names. Among them is *al-mubarak*, the blessing, because of the grace it brings to everyone who reads with an open heart and mind. Another is *al-shifa*, the curer, and some Muslims say they have been healed not only spiritually but also physically because they touched it with faith. It is also *al-nur*, the light. Spiritually it throws light; it shows up the shadows and lights the path to take; it also provides the light of knowledge, learning and understanding.

Education is important to Muslims and it begins with the Qur'an. Infants as young as four or five years old start to recite and children go to special schools in the mosque to learn Arabic.

Muslims find that the Qur'an is relevant even in the twenty-first century. It is not intended to be a text book but it is consistent with modern knowledge. For example, the poetry of the Quranic description of creation contains ideas consistent with scientific theories:

> *Do not the Unbelievers see that the heavens and the earth were joined together (as one Unit of Creation), before we clove them asunder? We made from water every living thing. Will they not then believe?*
>
> *And We have set on the earth mountains standing firm, lest it should shake with them, and We have made therein broad highways (between mountains) for them to pass through: that they may receive guidance.*
>
> *And We have made the heavens as a canopy well guarded: yet do they turn away from the Signs which these things (point to)!*
>
> *It is He Who created the Night and the Day, and the sun and the moon: all (the celestial bodies) swim along, each in its rounded course.*
>
> (Surah 21:30–33)

Muslims see the book as a miracle. The initial revelation was a miraculously dramatic event, the preservation of the book through the ages is amazing but most powerful of all is the effect it continues to have on the minds, hearts and souls of those who read it.

PRACTICE EXAMINATION QUESTIONS

1 (a) Describe how Muhammad ﷺ was given messages from Allah. (*8 marks*)

   Read the question carefully to make sure how much of the story is required. The encounter with Jibril in the cave Hira is necessary in some detail. Then in general describe the continuation of the revelation.

(b) Explain how and why Muslims show respect for the Qur'an. (*7 marks*)

   Address both how and why. The two may overlap. Remember that, besides marks of respect in the way the book is treated and its use in worship, there should be points about the practical application of its teaching in daily life. This is the opportunity to explain that the Qur'an has status and authority because it is a revelation from Allah.

(c) 'Islam would not exist without the Qur'an.' Do you agree? Give reasons to support your opinion and show you have thought about different points of view. (*5 marks*)

   Historically, the Qur'an has been an important factor in retaining the character of Islam. This might be a reason for agreeing with the quotation and evidence could be found to support the view. Others might see things differently. From a faith point of view Muslims might say that the will of Allah would have prevailed and the message could have been revealed some other way or they might feel that the statement is true and suggest reasons why the Qur'an provided the best means for creating and spreading Islam. The arguments can be historical, theological, philosophical or plain common sense – as long as you have considered other points of view and the evidence that might be used.

2 (a) Describe how Muslims use the Qur'an and the Hadith in their daily lives. (*8 marks*)

   Facts are required about the use of these two sources of guidance and it is sensible to define what the Qur'an and Hadith are in an introductory sentence but read ahead to the other parts of the question to see where best to put your points.

(b) Explain the difference between the status of the Qur'an and Hadith. (*7 marks*)

   The explanation should be about the authority of these two. The Qur'an is a revelation. The easiest way to explain the status of Hadith is to give a summary of why they were needed and how they came into being.

(c) 'Holy books should not be translated into modern languages.'
   Give reasons to support your opinion and show you have thought about different points of view. You must refer to Islam in your answer. (*5 marks*)

   You are free to agree or disagree but remember to include other points of view and to focus on the Qur'an in some of your answer. You may wish to consider the purpose of translation as part of your argument. The Hadith could be used in the discussion as illustration of points you are making. You are also expected to base your evidence on accurate information and sensitive understanding of Muslim attitudes towards sacred writings.

RELIGION, THE MEDIA AND ENTERTAINMENT

Knowledge of various issues and an understanding of them in the relationship between Religion, the Media and Entertainment. Knowledge of the religious basis for the issues raised

FOR DISCUSSION

- What do you think are the advantages and disadvantages of modern media?
- Which of these advantages and disadvantages might apply to Islam?

Media can be television, radio, videos, DVDs, CD-ROMS, newspapers, magazines, books, posters, advertisements, computers and the Internet, music, dance and drama, and sport. It can, in fact, be anything which is the medium for communicating with other people.

From the beginning of time, humans have given each other information, demonstrated new methods of doing things, passed on bright ideas, communicated their feelings, hopes and fears, made each other laugh and shared their opinions and beliefs. Every day in our modern world new ways of doing these things are developed.

In all religions and in all cultures there are some people who say that the popular media is a bad influence on life today and that young people especially are misled by the media and by modern forms of entertainment.

There are some religious people who welcome new inventions in the media and communication. They feel that modern technology will improve the quality of life for everyone and they see mass media as providing a wonderful opportunity to spread their beliefs.

There are, however, many religious people who have mixed feelings about the media and entertainment.

The film 'East is East' shows the life of some young Muslims in Britain

Before looking at specific issues concerning the media and entertainment, it is necessary to remember some basic Muslim beliefs:

- Muslims believe Allah is the one God. Allah and only Allah should be worshipped.
- Idolatry is forbidden; not simply the bowing down to images but also the making of any image.
- Humans were created for 'ibadah, worship of Allah.
- The material universe which Allah created is good and to be enjoyed.
- Humans are the khalifahs who look after the planet for Allah.
- There will be a day of Judgement.
- The Qur'an revealed to Muhammad ﷺ shows the straight way by which Allah wants people to live.
- Muslims must observe the Five Pillars.
- Jihad means striving to live correctly and working hard to establish Allah's rules in society.
- Allah judges people by their intentions.

THE ISSUES

Muslim attitudes to wealth follow logically from Muslim religious beliefs.

Muslims believe in Allah, the one God. Nothing else should be first in a Muslim's life. They certainly should not live for making money. To do so would be *shirk*, associating something else with Allah, the most serious sin of all.

There is nothing wrong in having wealth. It is not money but the attitude to money which causes problems.

> O ye who believe! Make not unlawful the good things which Allah hath made lawful for you, but commit no excess; for Allah loveth not those given to excess.
>
> (Surah 5:87)

Caring too much about material things is like worshipping false gods. Possessions can become like idols. It is said in many religions that you may think you own the possessions but in the end they own you. Even poor people could be guilty of making idols of things they want but cannot afford.

Everything Allah made is good. Muslims should enjoy life; they should be grateful for what Allah has given them and they should use it responsibly as good *khalifahs* or stewards. One of the Five Pillars is *zakat*, and this helps Muslims to budget their income and to develop sensible attitudes towards money and sharing (see Chapter 6).

Money (individuals' expenditure on the media) and the costs of the media; the influence of media on lifestyles.

Islam is a global religion. There are Muslims in over 120 countries. In Muslim countries, Islam in not only the majority religion but it is the basis of the laws of the country. Islamic beliefs and practices are part of the fabric of society. In such situations it may seem that freedom of choice is restricted but at least in some ways life is easier. In non-Muslim countries, especially in western countries like the United Kingdom, Muslims often have to make up their own minds about how to react to a secular lifestyle. Television is a good example of the problem.

Many Muslim families are concerned about the effect that television has on family life. Some see the TV set as being like a one-eyed idol in the corner of the living room, demanding attention and time. They feel that it has a bad effect on family life especially if families sit in front of the TV eating instead of making mealtimes a family occasion.

Muslims must beware not only of spending too much money but too much time on the media. Many people spend a lot of their leisure time

watching television and they could have been using this time to talk to each other or to do something more useful than simply sitting as a couch potato. For this reason, some Muslims refuse to own a television. Most Muslims in the United Kingdom do use the media but they believe that they need to choose carefully what to watch and read. Muslim parents are likely to try to make sure that their children only watch programmes or read magazines that are suitable for their age group and which do not promote the wrong values. Most parents would share this concern and try to monitor what their children watch, listen to and read. They are also likely to want to supervise their children when they use the Internet.

The media often present a view of the world that does not fit with Muslim beliefs about the priorities in life and the values people should live by.

Lifestyles portrayed in the media and advertising may have a bad effect particularly on impressionable young people or older people who are not well educated. In many drama series, for example, the main characters are married and divorced several times, have affairs and commit crimes. Even soap operas, supposedly about everyday life, have people burying bodies under the patio. The stories are interesting and entertaining but they give the impression that this is normal and acceptable behaviour.

FOR DISCUSSION

How far should any parents, not just Muslim parents, control the money and time which their children spend on the media?

For Muslims there is another factor which affects media issues. Making images of living things is forbidden in Islam. There are no statues nor pictures in a mosque. In some Islamic communities, the command against idolatry is taken so seriously that people refuse to have their photograph taken. For some Muslims this would be another reason for not having a television nor even a newspaper. Until recently in the United Kingdom educational text books about Islam, as a mark of respect for Muslim beliefs, would not have contained pictures of people. Some Muslims have now modified their traditional rules about this, but of course idolatry is still totally forbidden.

One problem for Muslims is that the media tends to make idols of people. Fame is big business. Film stars, pop stars and sports celebrities fill the media in the western world and it is very difficult, in particular for young people, to ignore popular culture.

Some aspects of popular culture are totally against the rules of Islam.

There will be at some future time people from my nation who will seek to make lawful, adultery, the wearing of silk by men, wine-drinking, and the use of musical instruments.

(Hadith)

Coolie Man is a Muslim rapper

Sufi Muslims dancing in a Turkish village

The regular use of alcohol is another feature of many dramas which might influence Muslims and lead them to stray from their faith. Many soap operas centre round the local pub.

Music is not a feature of religious worship in Islam and there are clear guidelines about what music is allowed. Most Muslims do not permit the use of musical instruments. However, in some Muslim countries there is a strong musical tradition. Sufi Muslims do a sacred dance.

Muslims may feel, however, that the pop music which bombards people in shops and stores may encourage unsuitable thoughts and actions.

ADVERTISING

It is not only the articles and the programmes which influence people. The adverts also affect people's attitudes. We are told that we will be happier, more successful, sexier or healthier if we buy a particular product and this might be anything from cigarettes to a new car.

Advertisements can be so subtle in their effect that there are terms invented to cover this aspect of their power: 'subliminal advertising' means the subconscious effect these 'hidden persuaders' might have. The aim is to make people buy things but it can have other unseen effects.

Advertising can encourage people to be greedy and to consume more than they really need. It can emphasise the differences between rich and poor and make people feel inadequate, envious and resentful. Many people, not only Muslims, feel that advertising promotes the wrong kind of values. It is part of a consumer society in which people judge others by what they own rather than what they are. Fashions and fads are encouraged by advertising so that people will tire of what they have and want something new. Some products are even made deliberately with a short life span so that they will wear out. This is called 'built-in obsolescence'.

CENSORSHIP – THE 'WATERSHED' – PORTRAYAL OF VIOLENCE AND SEX

Advertising serves a valuable function in telling the public what is available or what is new. Likewise, the media gives news and information. The Media and the advertising industry have codes of practice which are meant to protect the public. Also, laws of libel and slander stop the media telling total lies, though they cannot always control exaggeration and bias.

Very few people want to ban advertising and the media totally but there are many religious groups, including some Muslims, who petition the government or local authorities when they feel that a poster, an article, a book, a play or a film are offensive. Pressure groups try to influence the situation so that what has offended them is banned or censored.

Censorship can be a difficult issue. On the one hand people want to protect the vulnerable members of society. They fear, for example, that young children may be influenced to copy bad things they have seen. On the other hand there is the danger of eroding people's individual freedom. Freedom of speech and freedom of the press are important means of making sure that countries do not become dictatorships or police states.

The media has to effect a delicate balancing act. Newspapers and programmes need to provide what their readers and audience want but they must not offend other people. The watershed – nine o'clock at night – marks the time after which more explicit material can be shown on television. Many religious people campaign against sex and violence in the media and the watershed offers a compromise. Children are supposed to be in bed by that time and adults are capable of turning off the television if a programme causes offence.

Gratuitous sex and violence means showing sex and violence which is not necessary for the plot but which will attract a bigger audience. People make a lot of money from productions of pornographic material. Obviously this would be wrong in the eyes of many people, including Muslims.

For Muslims, violence and sex are not topics for viewing as entertainment. Islam is not a pacifist religion but even in a situation of war, the aim is ultimately to establish peace. Cruelty was spoken against by the Prophet. Even hurting people's feelings by back-biting and nagging is forbidden. In reality, there are always people who do not live up to the principles of their faith, whatever that faith might be.

Muslims believe that sex is a gift from Allah and they have strict rules which are intended to protect women. Pornography is wrong because it can give the impression that women exist to be used by men and it ignores the right purpose of sex.

Exploitation of women is a sensitive issue to Muslims. From the point of view of many Muslim women, it is western society which really exploits women. Scanty clothing and sexy behaviour seen in

Iranian pro-reformist women demonstrators, during the election campaign in Tehran, February 2000

much of the media offends many Muslims. The media meanwhile makes criticisms of the treatment of women in Islam. In Iran, part of the cultural revolution in 1979 after the Shah was deposed involved women once more becoming veiled. However, women in Iran now have a far greater say in the running of their society and almost half of the MPs in Iran are women. Western newspapers and television programmes tend to go for the most sensational stories that they can find about women in Islam. The issue is quite complex. By the year 2000 the daughters of many women who had welcomed the veil as a protest against western corruption were among the demonstrators in Tehran wanting reform.

The potential power of the media in political and religious issues is shown by the fact that e-mail petitions have been circulated in the West to protest about the treatment of women in several Muslim countries.

Western newspapers have carried stories that Saudi Arabia, a Muslim country, is censoring its citizens' use of the Internet. They have also carried stories that in the United Kingdom and in the United States some citizens (religious and secular)

have asked their Governments to restrict the availability of offensive material on the Internet.

THE RELATIONSHIP OF ISLAM TO THE MEDIA AND THE USE OF THE MEDIA BY MUSLIMS

In the United Kingdom, television and radio have always had an important role in bringing religious programmes and issues to the public. When the BBC started regular television broadcasting in 1946 it concentrated on religious programmes on Sundays between 10.30 a.m. and 12 noon and from 6.00 p.m. until 7 p.m. (2½ hours). These times became known as the 'God Slot' and were almost always entirely of Christian content. The programmes were often accused of presenting a cosy comfortable religion and they were seen as providing an opportunity for those who were housebound to join in worship. Many Christians and Muslims believe that religion is part of everyday life and they did not want religion pushed aside into a God slot. There were others who wanted the God slot as an opportunity to convert people. These are still topics for debate.

One of the issues in the United Kingdom is the

The Satanic Verses *caused offence to many Muslims*

matter of laws against blasphemy. Blasphemy consists of offensive or abusive remarks about God.

In the late 1980s, when Salman Rushdie wrote *The Satanic Verses* which caused offence to many Muslims, the Courts decided that, in England, blasphemy only offered protection to Christianity and possibly only to the Church of England. A related issue was how far authorities in Muslim countries had any right to declare a *fatwa* against Muslims living in non-Muslim countries. (A fatwa is a legal ruling by a pious, just and knowledgeable Muslim scholar or jurist, based on the Qur'an, Sunnah and Islamic Shari'ah.)

As the United Kingdom became more of a pluralist society, broadcasting has tried to reflect the changes in society. The BBC had always taken seriously the responsibility to educate. Educational TV and radio have covered multi-faith issues for many years. Nowadays the BBC and commercial stations have regular documentary programmes in popular time-slots on religious ethics and on the specific beliefs of various world faiths. Islam features regularly in such slots and many Muslims in the United Kingdom welcome the opportunity to explain their beliefs. They feel this will lessen prejudice, encourage more considerate treatment during times like Ramadan and encourage non-Muslims to find out more about the faith.

Increasingly, TV evangelism is seen on satellite and cable. Often these are American programmes, almost all made by Christians. Christians themselves in the United Kingdom have different opinions about such programmes. On the one hand believers want to share their faith with others and they were commanded to do so. On the other hand, religion is being marketed like a product and some feel it cheapens the religion. The United Kingdom has people of many faiths and it has usually been understood by the media that their purpose is not to convert people to any particular religion. It remains an issue for discussion especially since more and more TV channels are becoming available and the electronic revolution spreads further every day. People of no faith or of minority faiths may feel that their privacy is being invaded by religious broadcasting just as much as they sometimes get irritated by missionaries who come knocking at the door.

Islam, like Christianity, is a missionary faith. From the beginning Muhammad ﷺ urged his followers to write down the revelations. He wanted them to spread the message using the media of their time. Education begins with the Qur'an for Muslims.

In the United Kingdom the two faiths have tried to enter into dialogue with each other. Often they feel that they are on the same side and that secular materialism is the real enemy of both religions.

Some people feel that an important issue for all religions is not the impact of secular society and advertising but the popularising of New Age ideas in the media. Sometimes they mix and match anything about spirituality from various religions. Documentaries try to spice up the topics and fictional stories as a source of entertainment feature UFOs, angels and vampire slayers.

PREJUDICE AND DISCRIMINATION IN THE MEDIA

Prejudice means having an attitude, a pre-judged opinion, which is biased and not based on facts. Discrimination means the ability to distinguish between things. It has also come to mean an action which treats people unfairly on the basis of prejudice.

In Britain, the Race Relations Act 1976 makes it unlawful to discriminate against anyone on the grounds of race, colour, nationality or ethnic origin. It gives people the right to claim compensation for discrimination, harassment and victimisation. It applies to jobs, training, housing, education and the provisions of goods, facilities and services. Racial violence and other racial incidents are offences under criminal law. Inciting racial hatred is also a criminal

FOR DISCUSSION

- How biased do you think the media is about Islam? If you don't know, find out. Keep a record of articles in the press. Watch for bias.
- Humour is a difficult issue in the media. Do you think people should never be allowed to make fun of religion?

offence. However, racial prejudice cannot be made illegal because it is an attitude not an act. Laws cannot be made to censor people's thoughts.

The media has often been accused of racist attitudes by minority groups in the United Kingdom. It has also been accused of making fun of religion. Some Muslims accuse the media of both of these characteristics. More recently the media have been accused of Islamophobia. The term 'Islamophobia' is used to refer to hatred of Islam and of Muslims.

In 1997 a report called 'Islamophobia – a challenge for us all' was issued by the Runnymede Commission on British Muslims and Islamophobia. The report confirmed that many people in the United Kingdom have many prejudices about Islam. The media has been criticised for the part it has to play in openly or sometimes thoughtlessly perpetuating stereotypes. One example is that the media very rarely reflects the fact that there are many white Muslims and many well educated Muslims.

For many religions the presentation of religious figures and stories causes some problems but often the dramatisation or even the drawing of cartoons is thought to help children in particular to learn about the history and stories of a religion. The media can be helpful in catching people's interest in an entertaining way and it can be very educational.

The majority of Muslims have always taken literally the idea that there should be no representation of Allah nor of any living thing which Allah created. Even so, there were Islamic cultures which portrayed figures of people. They observed respectful traditions, however, such as covering the face of the Prophet with a cloth.

Arabic calligraphy

Calligraphy – beautiful writing from the Greek: *kallos* 'beauty' and *graphia* 'writing' – developed as an art form with the distinctive arabesque patterns of formalised leaves. It was never forgotten, even when making patterns, that Allah is the only creator, and sometimes a small flaw was left in the pattern to confirm this point. The Fatihah is the most calligraphed surah. It is often used for decoration of mosques and public buildings in Islamic countries.

With this background, it is not surprising that Muslims are cautious about representing the story of Islam on the screen. They are reluctant to do so themselves and they are opposed to non-Muslims doing so.

FOR DISCUSSION

- Should any restrictions be put on portraying religious leaders in the media?
- Do you think religious people can work in all parts of the media with a clear conscience?
- In which medium could Muslims best communicate their beliefs?

The message about the life of Muhammad ﷺ has never been shown on British television

Muslims do not worship the Prophet but they feel that portrayals of Muhammad ﷺ might be inaccurate and disrespectful. Films and books tend to add or omit parts of any story. Editing is necessary to make sense of the whole or to fit into a time-slot so any portrayal automatically becomes an interpretation. It can never be the whole truth. This is a dilemma that people in the media are always facing.

POLITICAL AND COMMERCIAL INTERESTS; THE CONTROL OF THE MEDIA.

Political and commercial interests control much of the world. The media can be the voice of the people. That is why the issues concerning the media are so important. The media in its many forms is part of our lives whether we like what it presents to us or not. The majority of Muslims realise that we cannot ignore it.

As well as sometimes being a bad influence on people, the media can uplift and encourage. It can help people to look at and consider moral, ethical and religious issues.

Islam is a way of life and Muslims believe that material things are to be used to the glory of Allah. True worship is made up of *iman* (belief) which is shown in *amal* (action) and is sustained by *ihsan* – the awareness of the presence of Allah.

It is not against Muslim beliefs to welcome the media and use the opportunities it provides.

Aid organisations can use the media to advertise their activities and encourage other people to get involved. This material is produced by Islamic Relief

GLOSSARY

A'isha One of the wives of the Prophet Muhammad ﷺ, and the daughter of Abu Bakr.

Abu Bakr The first Khalifah and the leader of the Muslim community after the death of the Prophet Muhammad ﷺ.

Abu Talib Uncle of the Prophet Muhammad ﷺ.

Adam The first man and the first Prophet of Allah.

Adhan The call to prayer.

Akhirah Everlasting life after death – the hereafter.

Al-Amin The trustworthy one. The name by which Prophet Muhammad ﷺ was known, even before the revelation of islam.

Al-Fatihah The Opening Surah 1 of the Qur'an. Recited at least 17 times daily during the five times of salah. Also known as 'The Essence' of the Qur'an.

'Ali Cousin and son-in-law of the Prophet Muhammad ﷺ, husband of Fatimah Zahrah; father of Hassan, Hussein, and Zainab, the fourth of the Rashidin according to Sunnis, and the first successor accepted by Shi'ah Islam.

Allah The name for God in Arabic. Allah is singular, has no plural, and is not associated with masculine, feminine or neuter characteristics.

Allahu Akbar Allah is most great.

Al-Madinah The name given to Hathrib after the Prophet Muhammad ﷺ migrated there in 622 CE and founded the first Islamic state.

Al-Masjid al-Haram Sharif The grand mosque in Makkah, which encompasses the Ka'bah, the hills of Safa and Marwah and the well of Zamzam.

Angels Beings created by Allah from light. They have no free will and are completely obedient to Allah.

Arafat A plain and hill, a few kilometres from Makkah, where pilgrims gather to worship, pray and ask for forgiveness on the 9th day of the month of Dhul-Hijjah, the day before Id-ul-Adha.

'Asr Mid-afternoon salah which may be performed from late afternoon until a short while before sunset.

Ayah 'Sign'. A unit within a Surah of the Qur'an.

Barakah Grace, blessings.

Bilal The first Mu'adhin, a companion of Prophet Muhammad ﷺ, and formerly an Abyssinian slave.

Bismillah In the name of Allah.

Bismillah-ir-Rahman-ir-Rahim In the name of Allah – All Gracious, All Merciful. This is the preface to all Surahs of the Qur'an except the 9th. It is usually said by Muslims before eating or beginning any action.

Dawud David. A Prophet of Allah to whom the Zabur (the Book of Psalms) was given.

Dhul-Hijah The month of the Hajj, last month of the Islamic year.

Du'a Various forms of personal prayer and supplication.

Fajr (Salat-ul-Fajr) Dawn salah which may be performed from dawn until just before sunrise.

Fard Obligatory duty according to divine law, e.g. offering salah five times a day.

Fatimah Daughter of the Prophet Muhammad ﷺ; wife of 'Ali, mother of Hassan, Hussein and Zainab.

Fatwa Legal guidance from a pious, just, knowledgeable Muslim scholar and jurist, based on the Qur'an, Sunnah and Islamic Shari'ah.

Fiqh Knowledge and understanding – a system of Islamic law.

Ghusi 'Greater ablution'. A ritual purifying shower prior to worship.

Hadith (pl. ahadith). A saying, report, or account. There are two types of Ahadith; the Prophetic and the Qudsi or Sacred. The Prophetic are wise sayings and advice which the Prophet gave. The Sacred sayings are in the words of Muhammad ﷺ but they are insights about the faith.

Hafiz (f. hafizah) Someone who knows the whole Qur'an by heart.

Hajar The wife of the Prophet Ibrahim, and mother of the Prophet Isma'il (peace be upon them).

Hajj The annual pilgrimage to Makkah, which each Muslim must undertake at least once in a lifetime if he or she has the health and wealth. A Muslim male who has completed Hajj is called Hajji, and a female, Hajjah.

Halal Any action or thing which is permitted or lawful.

Haram Any action or thing which is not permitted or unlawful.

Hijab Veil. Often used to describe the head scarf or modest dress worn by women, who are required to cover everything except face and hands in the sight of anyone other than immediate family.

Hijrah Departure; exit; emigration. The emigration of the Prophet Muhammad ﷺ from Makkah to al-Madinah in 622 CE. The Islamic calendar commences from this event.

Hira The name of a place near Makkah on a mountain called al-Nur, where the Prophet Muhammad ﷺ went for solitude and worship. It was there that he received the first revelation of the Qur'an.

'Ibadah All acts of worship. Any permissible action performed with the intention to obey Allah.

Iblis The Jinn who defied Allah by refusing to bow to Adam and later became the tempter of all human beings (see *Shaytan*).

Ibrahim (Abraham) A Prophet of Allah to whom the 'scrolls' were given.

Id Mubarak Id blessings! Greeting exchanged during Islamic celebrations.

Id Recurring happiness. A religious holiday; a feast for thanking Allah and celebrating a happy occasion.

Id-ul-Adja Celebration of the sacrifice, commemorating the Prophet Ibrahim's willingness to sacrifice his son Isma'il for Allah. Also known as Id-ul-Kabir – the Greater Id – and Qurban Bayram (Turkish) – feast of sacrifice.

Id-ul-Fitr Celebration of breaking the fast on the day after Ramadan ends, which is also the first day of Shawal, the tenth Islamic month. Also known as Id-ul-Saghir – the Lesser Id – and Sheker Bayram (Turkish) – sugar feast.

Ihram The state or condition entered into to perform either Hajj or Umrah. During this period, many normally permitted actions are out of bounds to Muslims. Ihram is also the name of the two plain white unsewn cloths worn by male pilgrims to indicate the brotherhood, equality and purity of the pilgrim. For women, Ihram clothing often consists of their normal modest dress.

Ijma' A general consensus of scholars, expressed or tacit, on matters of law and practice.

Imam A leader. A person who leads the communal prayer, or a founder of an Islamic school of jurisprudence. In Shi'ah Islam, Imam is also the title of 'Ali and his successors.

Iman Faith.

Injil Gospel, The book given to Prophet 'Isa.

'Iqamah Call to stand up for salah.

'Isa Jesus. A Prophet of Allah, born of the virgin Maryam.

'Isha' Evening salah which may be performed from just over an hour after sunset, until midnight.

Islam Peace attained through willing obedience to Allah's divine guidance.

Isma'il A Prophet of Allah. Son of the Prophet Ibrahim and Hajar.

Isnad Chain of transmission of each Hadith.

Jibril Gabriel. The angel who delivered Allah's messages to His Prophets.

Jihad A personal individual struggle against evil in the way of Allah. It can also be the collective defence of the Muslim community.

Jinn Being created by Allah from fire.

Jumu'ah (Salat-ul-Jumu'ah) The weekly communal salah, and attendance at the khutbah performed shortly after midday on Fridays.

Ka'bah A cube-shaped structure in the centre of the grand mosque in Makkah. The first house built for the worship of the One Time God.

Khadijah First wife of the Prophet Muhammad ﷺ. The mother of Fatimah Zahrah.

Khalifah Successor; inheritor; custodian; vice-regent.

Khutbah Speech. A talk delivered on special occasions such as the Jumu'ah and Id prayers.

Laylat-ul-Qadr The Night of Power, when the first revelation of the Qur'an was made to Prophet Muhammad ﷺ. It is believed to be one of the last ten nights of Ramadan.

Maghrib Sunset salah which is performed after sunset until daylight ends.

Mahdi Muhammad al-Muntazar. The (rightly) guided one who is awaited and will appear towards the end of time to lead the Ummah and restore justice on Earth.

Makkah City where the Prophet Muhammad ﷺ was born, and where the Ka'bah is located.

Maryam Mary. The virgin mother of the Prophet 'Isa.

Masjid Place of prostration. Mosque.

Mi'raj The ascent through the heavens of the Prophet Muhammad ﷺ.

Mihrab Niche or alcove in a mosque wall, indicating the Qiblah – the direction of Makkah, towards which all Muslims face to perform salah.

Mina Place near Makkah, where pilgrims stay on the 10th, 11th and 12th of Dhul-Hijjah and perform some of the activities of the Hajj.

Minbar Rostrum, platform, dais. The stand from which the Imam delivers the khutbah or speech in the mosque or praying ground.

Miqat Place appointed, at which pilgrims on the Hajj enter into the state of ihram.

Mu'adhin Caller to prayer (see *Adhan*). Known in English as 'muezzin'.

Muhammad ﷺ Praised. Name of the final Prophet ﷺ.

Muharram First month in the Islamic calendar, which is calculated from the time the Prophet Muhammad ﷺ migrated to Hathrib (Madinah).

Musa Moses. A Prophet of Allah to whom the Tawrah (Torah) was given.

Muslim Someone who claims to have accepted Islam by professing the Shahadah.

Muzdalifah Place where pilgrims on Hajj stop for a time during the night of the day they spend at Arafat.

Nabi Prophet of Allah.

Niyyah Intention. A legally required state of intent, made prior to all acts of devotion such as salah, Hajj or sawm.

Qadar Allah's complete and final control over the fulfilment of events or destiny.

Qiblah Direction which Muslims face when performing salah – towards the Ka'bah (see *Mihrab*).

Qur'an That which is read or recited. The Divine Book revealed to the Prophet Muhammad ﷺ. Allah's final revelation to humankind.

Rak'ah A unit of salah, made up of recitation, standing, bowing and two prostrations.

Ramadan The ninth month of the Islamic calendar, during which fasting is required from just before dawn until sunset, as ordered by Allah in the Qur'an.

Rashidin The Rightly Guided Khalifahs. The first four successors to the leadership role of the Prophet Muhammad ﷺ. They were Abu Bakr, 'Umar, 'Uthman and 'Ali.

Rasulullah Prophet of Allah.

Sa'y Walking and hastening between Safa and Marwah, as part of the Hajj, in remembrance of Hajar's search for water for her son Isma'il (peace be upon them).

Sadaqah Voluntary payment or good action for charitable purposes.

Safa and Marwah Two hills in Makkah, near the Ka'bah, now included within the grand mosque (see *Sa'y*).

Sahih. Sound. The title of the books of Hadith compiled by Abul Husayn Muslim ibn al-Hajjaj and Muhammad ibn Isma'il al-Bukhari, Sunni scholars. The collection is known as al-Sahihan – the Two Sahihs and described as Sahih (authentic).

Salah Prescribed communication with, and worship of Allah, performed under specific conditions, in the manner taught by the Prophet Muhammad ﷺ, and recited in the Arabic language. The five daily times of salah are fixed by Allah.

Sawm Fasting from just before dawn until sunset. Abstinence is required from all food and drink (including water) as well as smoking and conjugal relations.

Shahadah Declaration of faith, which consists of the statement, 'There is no god except Allah, Muhammad is the Messenger of Allah'.

Shari'ah Islamic law based upon the Qur'an and Sunnah.

Shaytan Rebellious; proud. The devil (see *Iblis*).

Shi'ah Followers. Muslims who believe in the Imamah, successorship of 'Ali after the Prophet Muhammad ﷺ and eleven of his most pious, knowledgeable descendants.

Shirk Association. Regarding anything as being equal or partner to Allah. Shirk is forbidden in Islam.

Sirah Biographic writings about the conduct and example of the Prophet Muhammad ﷺ.

Subhah String of beads used to count recitations in worship.

Sunnah Model practices, customs and traditions of the Prophet Muhammad ﷺ. This is found in both Hadith and Sirah.

Sunni Muslims who believe in the successorship of Abu Bakr, 'Umar, 'Uthman and 'Ali after the Prophet Muhammad ﷺ.

Surah Division of the Qur'an (114 in all).

Takbir Saying 'Allahu Akbar!' Recited during salah, Id and other celebratory occasions.

Tawaf Walking seven times around the Ka'bah in worship of Allah. Also, a part of Hajj and Umrah.

Tawhid Believe in the Oneness of Allah – absolute monotheism as practised in Islam.

Tawrah The Torah. The book given to the Prophet musa (Moses).

'Umar Second Khalifah of Islam.

'Uthman The third Khalifah of Islam.

Ummah Community. World-wide community of Muslims, the nation of Islam.

'Umrah Lesser pilgrimage which can be performed at any time of the year.

Wudu' Ablution before salah.

Yathrib Town to which the Prophet Muhammad ﷺ migrated from Makkah (see *al-Madina*).

Zabur The Book of Psalms given to Prophet Dawud (David).

Zakah Purification of wealth by payment of annual welfare due. An obligatory act of worship.

Zakat-ul-Fitr Welfare payment at the end of Ramadan.

Zamzam Name of the well adjacent to the Ka'bah in Makkah. The water first sprang in answer to Hajar's search and prayers (see *Hajar* and *Sa'y*).

Zuhr Salah which can be performed after midday until afternoon.

INDEX